HSC

ACPL ITEM
DISCARDED

510.285 M69r
Mitchell, R
Calculator
complete handbook

Y0-AAW-339

Contemporary's
CALCULATOR POWER

The Complete Handbook

- Computation
- Problem Solving
- Consumer Math
- Workplace Math

ROBERT MITCHELL

Project Editor:
Caren Van Slyke

Consultant:
Kenneth Tamarkin
Project Scale
Sommerville, Massachusetts

CB
CONTEMPORARY
BOOKS
CHICAGO

Library of Congress Cataloging-in-Publication Data

Mitchell, Robert, 1944–
    Calculator power : the complete handbook / Robert Mitchell.
       p.   cm.
    ISBN 0-8092-4197-8
    1. Calculators.   I. Title.
QA75.M58   1990
510′.285—dc20

90-2427
CIP

Allen County Public Library
Ft. Wayne, Indiana

Copyright © 1991 by Robert Mitchell
All rights reserved

No part of this publication may be reproduced, stored in
a retrieval system, or transmitted in any form or by any
means, without the prior written permission of the
publisher.

Published by Contemporary Books, Inc.
180 North Michigan Avenue, Chicago, Illinois 60601
Manufactured in the United States of America
International Standard Book Number: 0-8092-4197-8

Published simultaneously in Canada by
Fitzhenry & Whiteside
195 Allstate Parkway
Valleywood Business Park
Markham, Ontario L3R 4T8
Canada

Editorial Director
Caren Van Slyke

Editorial
Ellen Frechette
Pat Fiene
Karin Evans
Lisa Black
Scott Guttman
Larry Johnson
Lisa Dillman
Kathy Osmus

Editorial Production Manager
Norma Fioretti

Editorial Production
Jean Farley Brown
Marina Micari

Cover Illustrator
Daniel J. Hochstatter

Illustrators
John Hanley
Ophelia M. Chambliss-Jones

Art & Production
Lois Koehler

Typography
Impressions, Inc.
Madison, Wisconsin

CONTENTS

(continued)

About This Book

Calculator Power is specially designed to respond to the growing awareness of the value of calculators in the study of basic mathematics and to the increasing use of calculators and related devices in the lives of students, consumers, and employees. *Calculator Power* is based on five instructional goals:

- teaching calculator computation techniques

- helping students gain confidence by enhancing their problem-solving abilities

- showing students the importance of estimating—as a check on understanding as well as calculation accuracy

- highlighting calculator use in specific consumer and workplace situations

- addressing high-interest topics that frequently appear on the math sections of educational and vocational tests

Instructional material in *Calculator Power* is organized to be consistent with the order of topics found in most developmental math texts. For example, discussions of addition, subtraction, multiplication, and division of whole numbers follow one another on separate pages. Work with decimals is placed after work with whole numbers and is similarly organized according to the four basic operations. This enables you, the instructor, to coordinate instructional material in *Calculator Power* with your other instructional material for students of all levels.

Calculator Power focuses attention on the core skills common to the inexpensive calculators that most students will use. These skills involve the functions of addition, subtraction, multiplication, and division; the use of the percent and square-root keys; and the use of a four-key memory.

Calculator Power can be used in any of three ways:

- as an independent study text

- as a companion text for any basic math book

- as a reference text for basic calculator use

Calculator Power also features a detailed answer key so that students can check their own work and learn from their mistakes.

Hand-held calculators, as we know them today, are a relatively new invention. First appearing in the late 1960s, calculators initially were prohibitively expensive, costing as much as $1,500 each. By the mid-1970s, price reductions brought calculators within the reach of an average family budget. Today, a good four-function calculator can be purchased for just several dollars, comparable to the price of a short paperback book.

While the price of calculators has decreased, their use in schools has increased at all levels, from elementary school through high school. One result of the increasing availability of calculators in classrooms and in homes has been a renewed interest in their educational value. Educators generally find that students who use calculators tend to develop better problem-solving skills and computational abilities than students who don't use them.

To many teachers of mathematics, this is not a surprising discovery. When faced with word problems, many students suffer various degrees of "math anxiety." These students seem to be overwhelmed by the dual tasks of first unraveling a word problem and then doing a correct computation—even though both skills may be within their abilities. By minimizing computation anxiety, using a calculator may enable students to more fully concentrate on problem-solving skills. Improvement in problem-solving skills, in turn, often results in a better attitude toward mathematics in general, accompanied by noticeable improvement in overall computational abilities, with or without the use of a calculator.

Calculators are also becoming more important in the workplace and in the home. Because of this, vocational training now usually includes instruction in the use of a calculator or in a related device such as a cash register. And, of particular interest to students, many educational and pre-employment tests check an applicant's skill with a calculator. Additionally, the ability to use a calculator can enhance an individual's efficiency and effectiveness on the job.

In response to the growing importance of calculators in modern life, and encouraged by the results of educational research, the National Council of Teachers of Mathematics has formally endorsed the use of calculators in classrooms, stating that mathematics teachers "should recognize the potential contribution of the calculator as a valuable instructional aid" and prescribing that the calculator "should be used in imaginative ways to reinforce learning and to motivate the learner as he or she becomes proficient in mathematics."

Welcome to Calculator Power

Calculator Power is designed to help you master the use of a hand-held calculator for all types of basic math problems. You will learn to use a calculator to add, to subtract, to multiply, and to divide. You'll discover how a calculator can simplify your work with whole numbers, decimal numbers, fractions, and percents. And you'll learn how a calculator can help you gain confidence in solving word problems and in working with geometry and algebra.

Several features of *Calculator Power* will help make using a calculator more enjoyable. As shown below, many of these features are identified by special symbols that appear on pages throughout the book.

Step-by-step examples show how to use a calculator to solve math problems you're most likely to come across in daily life and on tests—whether educational tests or employment tests.

The Discovery features include interesting calculator or math tips that will improve your work.

Pencil-and-paper exercises increase your understanding of calculator use.

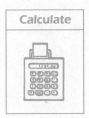

Calculator exercises give you practice using a calculator for a wide range of math problems.

Mental Calculation exercises improve your ability to estimate answers. Estimating helps you see how to solve a problem or how to catch yourself when you make a mistake on the calculator.

Spotlight on Consumers pages highlight uses of a calculator especially important to you in your daily-life role as a consumer.

Spotlight on the Workplace pages focus on uses of a calculator especially important at the workplace.

Fun with Your Calculator pages contain enjoyable games that challenge your calculator skills.

To get the most out of your work, do each exercise carefully. Check your answers as you finish each page. The answer key starts on page 127.

PART 1

Becoming Familiar with Calculators

To *calculate* is to work with numbers. You calculate each time you add, subtract, multiply, or divide. You can calculate "in your head," with paper and pencil, or by using a calculator.

In this section, you will learn the basics of calculator use.

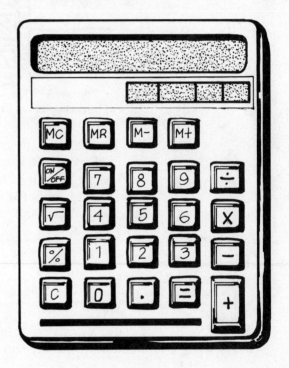

A **calculator** is an electronic device that makes it easy to work with numbers. When used carefully, a calculator is amazingly quick and accurate. The calculator pictured below may be similar to one you own or use.

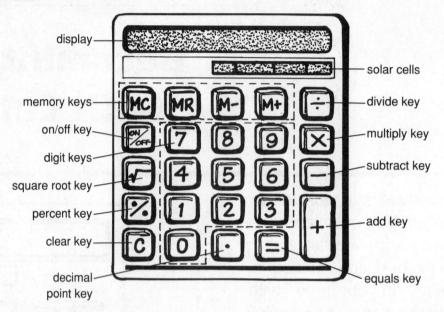

You'll soon learn about all the keys shown above. For now, notice the group of ten **digit keys:** (0), (1), (2), (3), (4), (5), (6), (7), (8), and (9). Digit keys let you enter numbers on a calculator. Entering a number is similar to dialing a number on a touch-tone telephone. You simply press one digit at a time.

Write

Choose a drawing below and fill in the keys as they are placed on your calculator. Modify the drawing as needed.

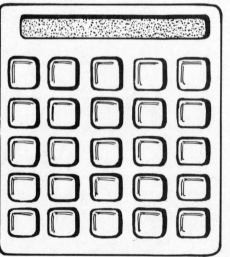

Battery Powered

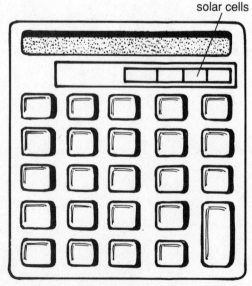

Solar Powered

In this book, you will learn about **four-function, four-key memory calculators**.

- The four **function keys** are labeled $\boxed{+}$, $\boxed{-}$, $\boxed{\times}$, and $\boxed{\div}$.
- The four **memory keys** are labeled $\boxed{M+}$, $\boxed{M-}$, $\boxed{MR}$, and $\boxed{MC}$.

Solar-Powered Calculators

A **solar-powered** calculator contains a row of solar cells. These cells change light into electricity to make the calculator work. You can distinguish solar cells from a display (where the numbers appear) by the cells' darker color.

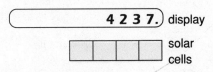

Don't expect to see numbers appear on the solar cells! The cells' only purpose is to change light into electricity. A solar-powered calculator won't work in a dimly lit room.

Most solar-powered calculators have an ON key and an OFF key. Others simply have a cover that opens and closes to turn the calculator on and off.

Battery-Powered Calculators

A **battery-powered** calculator contains a battery—usually placed in the back of the calculator.

All battery-powered calculators have an ON key and an OFF key. On some calculators, these two functions are performed by a single ON/OFF key.

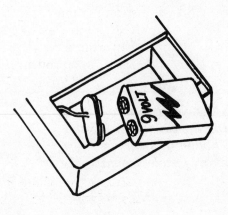

9V Battery

The Calculator Display

Most calculators display the value "0." when they are turned on. If your calculator does not display a 0 when you press the ON key, your calculator has a problem:

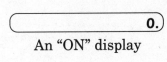

An "ON" display

- A solar-powered calculator may have a problem with its solar cells. You should return this calculator to the store.
- A battery-powered calculator may have a dead battery. Or someone may have forgotten to put a battery in!

The largest number a calculator can work with is determined by the size of its display. Most calculators have an 8-digit display.

$\boxed{2\ 4\ 8\ 5\ 7\ 3\ 9\ 4.}$

A displayed 8-digit number

Because everyone makes mistakes, calculators have special erasing keys called **clear keys.** Different calculators use different clear key symbols. However, most calculators use one or two of the keys described below.

Learn the meaning of the one or two clear keys that are on your calculator. Just familiarize yourself with the others.

Key	Meaning	Function
(C)	Clear	The *Clear* key erases the display and may also erase all parts of a calculation stored in the calculator.
(ON/C)	On/Clear	Pressing (ON/C) turns the calculator on and erases the display.
(CE)	Clear Entry	A *Clear Entry* key erases the display only.
(CE/C)	Clear Entry/Clear	Pressing (CE/C) once clears the display. Pressing (CE/C) twice clears both the display and other parts of a calculation stored in the calculator.
(AC)	All Clear	An *All Clear* key erases all numbers and functions stored in a calculator.

Discovery

On most calculators, you can also clear the display by turning the calculator off and then on again. Though it is not recommended, many people use this technique.

Calculate

Answer each of the following questions about your calculator.
1. Is your calculator solar powered or battery powered?
2. Which key do you press (if any) to turn your calculator on?
3. When turned on, what appears on your calculator's display?
4. After turning your calculator on, press the whole number keys in order: (1), (2), (3), (4), (5), (6), (7), (8), and (9). How many digits appear on your calculator display?
5. Which key do you press to erase your calculator's display?
6. What is the largest number you can display on your calculator?

The Decimal Point Key

The ⊙ key is the **decimal point** key. When you enter an amount of money, you use a decimal point to separate dollars from cents. Cents appear in the first two places to the right of the decimal point.

For example:

$14.29

number of dollars ⎯⎤ ⎡⎯ number of cents

decimal point

Here are some points to remember:

- No dollar sign is displayed on a calculator.
  The amount $14.29 is entered as ①④⊙②⑨ and is displayed as

  ⎽⎽⎽⎽⎽⎽⎽1 4 . 2 9⎽

- When you enter cents only, the calculator displays a 0 to the left of the decimal point.
  The amount $.18 is entered as ⊙①⑧ and is displayed as

  ⎽⎽⎽⎽⎽⎽⎽0 . 1 8⎽

- When you enter an amount between 1¢ and 9¢, put a 0 between the decimal point and the cents digit.
  On a calculator, you enter $3.08 as ③⊙⓪⑧ .

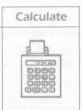

Calculate

On your calculator, enter each of the following money amounts. Then, below each amount, write how that value appears on the calculator display. (Clear the display before each entry.)

1. $2.57 $17.81 $20.56 $.49 $.08 $.10
   2. 5 7

2. four dollars and nineteen cents   six dollars and twelve cents

3. twenty-seven cents   forty-two cents

4. four cents   eight cents

5. one dollar and six cents   two dollars and seven cents

Think for a moment about things you've discovered about a calculator:

- Digit keys are used to enter numbers.

- You enter a number one digit at a time, starting with the left-hand digit.

- You can set the display to "0" by pressing a clear key.

- You press the decimal point key (·) to separate dollars from cents.

Here's another interesting fact: A calculator does not have a comma (,) key.

For example, to enter 1,960, you press (1)(9)(6)(0). **You do not enter a comma.**

Example 1

To enter 8,250 on your calculator, press keys as shown at the right.

Press Keys	Display Reads
8	8.
2	8 2.
5	8 2 5.
0	8 2 5 0.

Discovery

Calculators display a decimal point to the right of a whole number.
- *Most calculators do not display a comma.*
- *If they do, the comma **may** be at the top of the number as in Example 2.*

Example 2

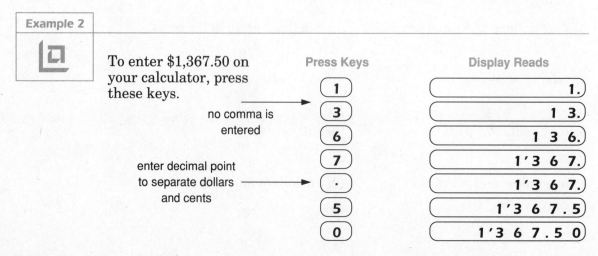

To enter $1,367.50 on your calculator, press these keys.

no comma is entered →

enter decimal point to separate dollars and cents →

Press Keys	Display Reads
1	1.
3	1 3.
6	1 3 6.
7	1'3 6 7.
·	1'3 6 7.
5	1'3 6 7.5
0	1'3 6 7.5 0

A. Rewrite all of the numbers. Be sure to write each number larger than 999 with a comma. The first is completed as an example.

no decimal point

1. (2 4 5 0.) 2,450 ↙
2. (8 7 5.) _____
3. (4 0 5 6.) _____

4. (3 9 4 5 0.) _____
5. (1 8 3 2.) _____
6. (2 9 6 0 9.) _____

B. Write these money amounts with a dollar sign and a comma, if needed.

1. (1 8.3 2) $18.32 _____
2. (2 4 7 1.6 0) _____

3. (6 4 9.0 9) _____
4. (5 0 3 8.1 8) _____

C. Choose how each of the displayed numbers and money amounts would be written.

1. (3 4 0.)
   a) thirty-four
   b) three hundred forty
   c) three thousand, four hundred

3. (3.0 7)
   a) thirty-seven cents
   b) three dollars and three cents
   c) three dollars and seven cents

2. (9 0 0.)
   a) nine
   b) ninety
   c) nine hundred

4. (0.2 0)
   a) twenty cents
   b) two dollars
   c) twenty dollars

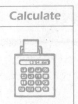

D. Enter each of the following numbers on your calculator. Write how each displayed number looks. Be sure to write in the decimal point.

1. ninety-five   (9 5.)

2. two hundred forty-three   (   )

3. three thousand, five hundred twenty-nine (   )

4. eight thousand, four hundred six   (   )

5. fifteen dollars and eighty-two cents   (   )

6. two hundred four dollars and nine cents   (   )

MAKING THE DISPLAY SPEAK!

On this page we'll show you a fun and creative game that can be played on a calculator. It might be an interesting introduction to calculators for you or someone you know.

Calculate

1. On your calculator, see if you can discover what letter of the alphabet each digit most closely resembles when viewed upside down. Turn the calculator upside down, punch in the numbers, and fill in the letters you see.

   Calculator digit   **0 1 2 3 4 5 6 7 8**

   Letter resembled by   __ __ __ E __ __ __ __ __
   upside-down digit

2. In the English alphabet, the vowels are *a, e, i, o, u,* and sometimes *y.* What are the three vowels in the upside-down calculator alphabet that you just did? __ __ __

3. What word can be read on an upside-down display when each of the following numbers is entered?
   14 _____ **345** _____ **710** _____

4. Make a list of four two-letter words that can be written with "calculator letters." (Hint: Each word contains 1 vowel.)

5. Make a list of five three-letter words that can be written with "calculator letters."

PART 2

Whole Numbers and Money

Much of the math we do involves whole numbers and money. Calculators can help us work more effectively with large numbers and with large groups of whole numbers. Calculators can also help us focus our efforts on thinking about how to solve problems.

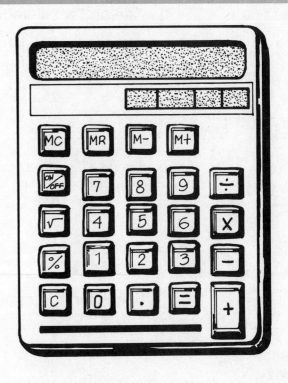

The Add Key and the Equals Key

The $+$ key is called the **add key** and is used to add numbers. The $=$ key is called the **equals key** and, when pressed, tells a calculator to display the answer to a calculation.

To see how the $+$ key and the $=$ key work together in a calculation, press the following keys in order:

What answer does your calculator display show? _____

Adding Two Numbers

If your calculator displayed 8, you already know how to add two numbers! (Remember to clear your calculator display before beginning each new problem.)

Example 1

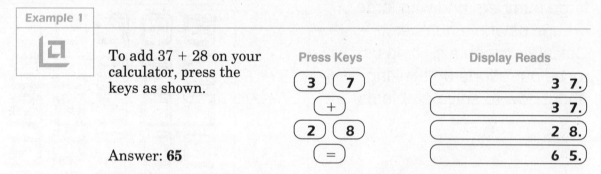

To add 37 + 28 on your calculator, press the keys as shown.

Press Keys	Display Reads
3 7	3 7.
+	3 7.
2 8	2 8.
=	6 5.

Answer: **65**

Reminder: Clear your calculator display before you start a new problem.

Discovery
- *Most displays do not show a + sign.*
- *The answer appears only after you press $=$.*

Example 2

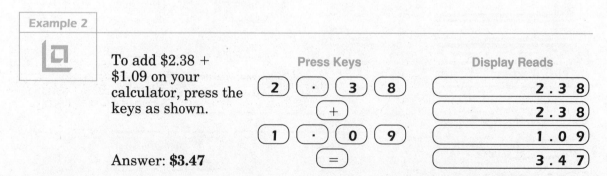

To add $2.38 + $1.09 on your calculator, press the keys as shown.

Press Keys	Display Reads
2 . 3 8	2 . 3 8
+	2 . 3 8
1 . 0 9	1 . 0 9
=	3 . 4 7

Answer: **$3.47**

A. Fill in the numbers and operations to show what keys you would press to solve each problem. **Do not write the solution.**

1. 8 + 4 =   ⟨ 8 ⟩⟨ + ⟩⟨ 4 ⟩⟨ = ⟩

2. 39 + 17 =   ⟨ ⟩⟨ ⟩⟨ ⟩⟨ ⟩⟨ ⟩

3. 2,063 + 989 =   ⟨ ⟩⟨ ⟩⟨ ⟩⟨ ⟩⟨ ⟩⟨ ⟩⟨ ⟩

4. $5.09 + $4.26 =   ⟨ ⟩⟨ ⟩⟨ ⟩⟨ ⟩⟨ ⟩⟨ ⟩⟨ ⟩⟨ ⟩

5.   128
     + 89   ⟨ ⟩⟨ ⟩⟨ ⟩⟨ ⟩⟨ ⟩⟨ ⟩

6. $7.90
     + 3.78   ⟨ ⟩⟨ ⟩⟨ ⟩⟨ ⟩⟨ ⟩⟨ ⟩⟨ ⟩⟨ ⟩

7. thirty-five plus fourteen
     ⟨ ⟩⟨ ⟩⟨ ⟩⟨ ⟩⟨ ⟩

8. the sum of one hundred fifty-seven and sixty-one
     ⟨ ⟩⟨ ⟩⟨ ⟩⟨ ⟩⟨ ⟩⟨ ⟩

9. five thousand, two hundred nine plus two thousand, four hundred
     ⟨ ⟩⟨ ⟩⟨ ⟩⟨ ⟩⟨ ⟩⟨ ⟩⟨ ⟩

10. four dollars and fifty cents added to six dollars and twelve cents
     ⟨ ⟩⟨ ⟩⟨ ⟩⟨ ⟩⟨ ⟩⟨ ⟩⟨ ⟩

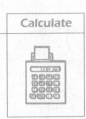
B. Solve each of the following problems on your calculator.

1. 41 + 18 =   450 + 207 =   1,950 + 872 =

2. $.98 + $.67 = $34.09 + $20.98 = $245.75 + $169.99 =

3. What is the combined weight of the pickup and trailer?

3,875 pounds   1,543 pounds

KEYING ERRORS

Called **keying errors,** calculator errors are very common. In fact, keying errors are so common that we want to take this page to alert you to them!

There are three main types of keying errors:

- pressing the wrong key
  Example: Pressing (8) (2) instead of (9) (2).

- double keying—accidentally pressing the same key twice
  Example: Pressing (4) (7) (7) instead of (4) (7).

- transposing digits—pressing keys in the wrong order
  Example: Pressing (3) (5) instead of (5) (3).

As you practice your calculator skills throughout this book, be careful to avoid each type of keying error.

Write

For each problem below, indicate by a check (✔) which type of error was made. Then, fill in the blank keys to show the correct way to key each problem.

A. Problem to Solve	Keys Pressed	B. Wrong Key	Double Keying	Transposed Digits
1. 27 + 18	(2)(7)(+)(1)(1)(8)(=)	_____	_____	_____
Correct:	( )( )( )( )( )			
2. $39 + $26	(3)(9)(+)(6)(2)(=)	_____	_____	_____
Correct:	( )( )( )( )( )			
3. 153 + 89	(1)(4)(3)(+)(5)(9)(=)	_____	_____	_____
Correct:	( )( )( )( )( )( )			
4. $.67 + $.49	(·)(7)(6)(+)(·)(4)(9)(=)	_____	_____	_____
Correct:	( )( )( )( )( )( )( )			
5. $85 + $32	(8)(5)(−)(3)(2)(=)	_____	_____	_____
Correct:	( )( )( )( )( )( )			

DECIDING WHEN TO USE A CALCULATOR

Try the experiment below. There are 24 problems, divided into three types. Try doing each problem the easiest way for you:

- in your head
- with paper and pencil, or
- with a calculator.

When you've finished all 24 problems, indicate the way you preferred to do each problem. Write the numbers of the problems on the lines.

Type A: Single-Digit Addition

1. $6 + 0 =$ **3.** $4 + 5 =$ **5.** $3 + 4 =$ **7.** $2 + 6 =$

2. $9 + 4 =$ **4.** $3 + 8 =$ **6.** $7 + 6 =$ **8.** $8 + 9 =$

Type B: Double-Digit Addition

9. $30 + 20 =$ **11.** $51 + 46 =$ **13.** $75 + 24 =$ **15.** $72 + 16 =$

10. $52 + 39 =$ **12.** $46 + 28 =$ **14.** $57 + 49 =$ **16.** $86 + 47 =$

Type C: Triple-Digit Addition

17. $\begin{array}{r} 348 \\ + 121 \\ \hline \end{array}$ **19.** $\begin{array}{r} 635 \\ + 122 \\ \hline \end{array}$ **21.** $\begin{array}{r} 563 \\ + 316 \\ \hline \end{array}$ **23.** $\begin{array}{r} \$4.23 \\ + 2.45 \\ \hline \end{array}$

18. $\begin{array}{r} 658 \\ + 469 \\ \hline \end{array}$ **20.** $\begin{array}{r} 797 \\ + 328 \\ \hline \end{array}$ **22.** $\begin{array}{r} \$886 \\ + 527 \\ \hline \end{array}$ **24.** $\begin{array}{r} \$6.93 \\ + 4.58 \\ \hline \end{array}$

In your head: _____

Pencil and paper: _____

Calculator: _____

Why do you think some problems are more easily done **without** the use of a calculator? Write your reasons below.

_____

_____

_____

_____

A calculator combines 3 or more numbers by adding 2 at a time.

Example 1

Add 9 + 8 + 6

Press Keys	Display Reads	
9	9.	
+	9.	
8	8.	
+	1 7.	← subtotal of 9 + 8
6	6.	
=	2 3.	← total of 17 + 6

Answer: **23**

Discovery

Most calculators display a subtotal each time a (+) is pressed. A subtotal is the total of numbers added up to the point where the (+) key is pressed.

Does your calculator display subtotals? To find out, try Example 1 on your calculator.

Example 2

Add

$24.87
12.99
+   8.35

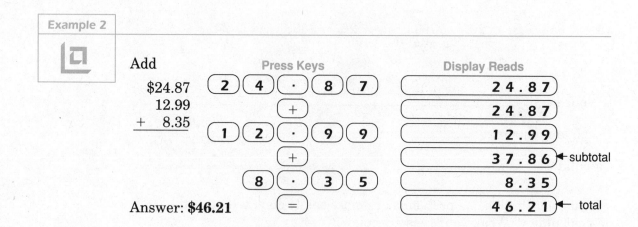

Press Keys	Display Reads	
2 4 · 8 7	24.87	
+	24.87	
1 2 · 9 9	12.99	
+	37.86	← subtotal
8 · 3 5	8.35	
=	46.21	← total

Answer: **$46.21**

A. Fill in the key symbols at right to show how to solve each problem
—using the $\boxed{=}$ key only once. Problem 1 is completed for you.
Do not write the solution.

1. $12 + 9 + 8 =$ ⟨1⟩⟨2⟩⟨+⟩⟨9⟩⟨+⟩⟨8⟩⟨=⟩

2. $35 + 27 + 9 =$ ⟨ ⟩⟨ ⟩⟨ ⟩⟨ ⟩⟨ ⟩⟨ ⟩⟨ ⟩

3. $\$1.53 + \$.94 + \$.58 =$ ⟨ ⟩⟨ ⟩⟨ ⟩⟨ ⟩⟨ ⟩⟨ ⟩⟨ ⟩
⟨ ⟩⟨ ⟩⟨ ⟩⟨ ⟩

B. Solve each of the following problems on your calculator.

1. $45 + 27 + 8 =$ $\$5.67 + \$.25 + \$.79 =$ $75 + 47 + 29 =$

2.
73	$3.59	154	$245	$125.75
28	2.89	83	171	87.50
+ 9	+ .78	+ 99	+ 128	+ 69.99

3. While shopping Saturday, Amanda
bought the three items shown at right.
What was the total cost of these items?

$3.98

$2.89

$5.85

C. A student used a calculator to solve the following problems. Because
of "keying errors," four of the problems have **wrong answers.**
Without using a calculator or pencil, spot the four problems with
wrong answers. Then, use your calculator to find correct answers.

1.
28
17
+ 9
54

3.
$8.43
3.57
+ .98
$12.89

5.
231
106
+ 53
290

7.
$6.90
8.23
+ 4.50
$19.63

2.
354
227
+ 100
681

4.
$365
154
+ 116
$935

6.
$28.90
17.83
+ 13.58
$60.31

8.
5,675
1,476
+ 850
2,794

The (−) key is called the **subtract key** and is used to subtract one number from another.

Example 1

To subtract 37 from 108 on your calculator, press keys as shown.

Press Keys	Display Reads
1 0 8	1 0 8.
−	1 0 8.
3 7	3 7.
=	7 1.

Answer: **71**

More than one number can be subtracted by pressing (−) before each new subtraction. Press (=) only once, after you enter the final number.

Reminder: Clear your calculator display before you start a new problem.

Example 2

Solve the following word problem.

Stan paid $11.98 for a hammer plus $.60 tax. How much change did Stan get from a $20 bill?

To solve, subtract each amount from $20.

Press Keys	Display Reads
2 0 · 0 0	2 0.0 0
−	2 0.0 0
1 1 · 9 8	1 1.9 8
−	8.0 2
· 6 0	.6 0
=	7.4 2

Answer: **$7.42**

Note: When you have numbers like $20, you can enter 20.00 or just 20 on your calculator. Many people prefer to enter all of the 0's as a reminder that they are working with dollars and cents.

Discovery

Try the following subtraction problem on your calculator: **You subtract** **The display reads**

$.35 − $.15   [0.2]

The answer is $.20, but the display reads 0.2. This example shows another feature of calculators:

- *A calculator does not display a 0 that is at the right-hand end of the decimal part of an answer.*

- *When you write down an answer in money, remember to add this zero* ⟶

  $0.2 $0.20
  no   yes

A. Fill in the numbers and operations to show what keys you would press to solve each problem. **Do not write the solution.**

1. fifty-nine minus twenty-eight

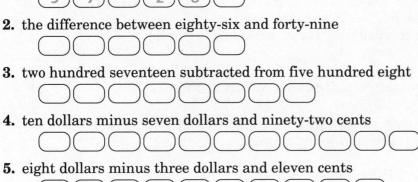

(5)(9)(−)(2)(8)(=)

2. the difference between eighty-six and forty-nine

◯◯◯◯◯◯

3. two hundred seventeen subtracted from five hundred eight

◯◯◯◯◯◯◯◯

4. ten dollars minus seven dollars and ninety-two cents

◯◯◯◯◯◯◯◯◯◯

5. eight dollars minus three dollars and eleven cents

◯◯◯◯◯◯◯◯◯

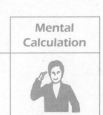

Mental Calculation

B. Keying errors led one student to three **incorrect** answers below. See if you can find them. Then check your work with your calculator.

| **1.** 27
− 9
36 | **2.** 107
− 79
28 | **3.** 422
− 106
88 | **4.** $20.00
− 12.49
$7.51 | **5.** $124.00
− 82.46
$206.46 |

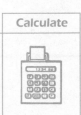

Calculate

C. Solve each of the following problems on your calculator.

1. 9 − 7 =   23 − 8 =   65 − 49 = $1.45 − $.85 =

2. 47 − 23 − 9 =   119 − 57 − 28 =   231 − 103 − 37 =

3. $20.00 − $13.89 − $3.19 = $25.00 − $9.08 − $4.52 =

4. As pictured at right, how many pounds heavier is the van than the sports car?

4,138 pounds   2,869 pounds

5. Mari paid for her lunch, shown at right, with a 10-dollar bill. If her tax is $.18, how much change should Mari be given?

Coffee
$.75

Ham & Cheese Sandwich
$2.45

Have you ever thought, "Wow, that calculator is really smart!" You're not alone if you have!

Yet, amazing as it is, a calculator can't tell you:

- which numbers are important
- whether to add or to subtract
- whether the answer you compute is correct

Problem-Solving Steps for Word Problems

When solving word problems, you may find it useful to follow the five-step problem-solving approach:

Step 1. Determine what the question asks you to find.
Step 2. Decide what numbers are needed to answer the question.
Step 3. Choose the operation (addition, subtraction, multiplication, or division) you wish to use.
Step 4. Solve the problem by doing the math and answering the question.
Step 5. Read the question again and see if your answer makes sense.

Mental Calculation

Nathan traded in his Ford on a new Honda. Although the sticker price was $13,450, the salesman lowered this price by $2,875. Nathan was also given a trade-in allowance of $2,250, although the Ford was only worth $1,800. Using his trade-in as a down payment, how much did Nathan still owe on the Honda?

A. Decide whether "mental skills" or "calculator skills" are most important in helping you answer each question below about the word problem. Circle your choice.

1. What are you asked to find? mental skills calc. skills

2. Which three of the following numbers are needed to answer the question? mental skills calc. skills

   $13,450 $2,875 $2,250 $1,800

3. Do you add or subtract the numbers you chose in question 2? mental skills calc. skills

4. What answer results from each addition or subtraction you perform? mental skills calc. skills

5. Does your answer make sense? mental skills calc. skills

Carefully read word problems A and B, and do the exercise that follows.

A. Last weekend, Hamburger Heaven sold $843 worth of hamburgers, $257 worth of fries, and $385 worth of drinks. How much money did Hamburger Heaven take in on these three products last weekend?

B. Last weekend, Hamburger Heaven sold $50 worth of hamburgers, $20 worth of fries, and $30 worth of drinks. How much money did Hamburger Heaven take in on these three products last weekend?

Mental Calculation

B. For questions 1 and 2, check (✔) the one answer that most closely expresses your opinion.

1. Which problem above, A or B, seems more difficult?
   A _____   B _____   About the same _____

2. If you checked A or B above, why do you think that problem was more difficult than the other?
   _____ Different situations are described.
   _____ The harder problem contains larger numbers.
   _____ The harder problem is longer.

If you're like most students, you think problem A is more difficult. Why? Most likely because it contains larger numbers.

This is a natural way to feel. After all, we usually think that larger numbers are harder to work with than smaller numbers.

> By using a calculator, you can concentrate on solving the problem. All types of numbers—large and small—become easier to work with.

Here's how to practice doing word problems using a calculator:

- Read a problem for understanding.
- Concentrate on problem-solving steps 1, 2, 3, and 5 listed on page 18.
- Have confidence you can do any calculation correctly.

Write

C. In your own words, tell why you think a calculator can help you become a better word-problem solver.

_____

_____

_____

Herald Gazette

Read All About It!
Math Common Sense Rescues Shopper

Lilly Sharp foiled a bugged calculator yesterday when she was overcharged $24.82. Saved by her common sense, Sharp yelled "THIEF!" at the dumbfounded clerk. Knowing her bill should be about $15.00, Sharp was heard to exclaim, "I can spot a calculator error a mile away!" Much to the clerk's embarrassment, Sharp received a loud round of applause from other excited shoppers!

Lilly Sharp may be fictional, but her story illustrates an important fact.

- Being able to spot an incorrect answer is a very valuable skill.

Sometimes you can spot a wrong answer by using **math intuition.** Other times it helps to use a method called **estimation** (also called **approximation**).

- Math intuition, or "math common sense," is a feeling about what an answer should be. Math intuition told Lilly that a few groceries couldn't cost $74.82.
- To estimate is to compute an approximate answer. To find an estimate, you use round numbers that are easy to work with.

Here's an example: On another occasion, Lilly paid for a $28.63 purchase with a $50.00 bill. Is $12.37 a reasonable amount of change?

Lilly's intuition told her that $12.37 was not enough! She estimated to make sure: She thought, "$28.63 is about $30, and $50 − $30 is $20. My change should be about $20!"

As Lilly discovered, the best protection against calculator error is the ability to spot a wrong answer. And estimating is your most helpful tool.

Throughout the rest of this book, you'll use estimation to check calculator answers. By using estimation to catch keying errors, you'll learn to use a calculator accurately and confidently.

- Whenever possible, you should do estimates with pencil and paper or in your head.

To estimate, replace each number in a problem with a **round number.**
A round number has zeros to the right of a chosen place value. (10s,
100s, 1000s, etc.)

For example, $30.00 is a round number for the value $28.63.

Example

Mental
Calculation

Find an estimated answer for the
addition problem at right.

To do this, round each number to
the nearest 100, and then add.

Problem	Estimate
912	900
786	800
+ 328	+ 300
2,026 ◄ close ►	2,000

A. Estimate an answer to each problem by rounding as indicated. Give
only the estimated answer.

In row 1, round each number to the nearest 10.

	Estimate		**Estimate**		**Estimate**
1. 89	90	48	5̶6̶	9̶2̶	9̶0̶
+ 72	+ 70	+ 33	3̶0̶	− 41	4̶0̶
	160		8̶1̶ 8̶0̶	51	3̶0̶ 5̶0̶

In row 2, round each number to the nearest 100.

	Estimate		**Estimate**		**Estimate**
2. 488	500	897		$724	
− 213	− 200	+ 108		− 336	
	300				

In row 3, round each number to the nearest 1,000.

	Estimate		**Estimate**		**Estimate**
3. 4,927	5,000	7,849		12,193	
+ 2,083	+ 2,000	+ 4,906		− 7,826	
	7,000				

B. Find the best estimate for the answer to each problem below. Match
the letter of the best estimate on the line to the left of each problem.

Computation Problems	Estimates
_____ **1.** 38 + 54 40	**a)** 50
_____ **2.** 92 − 33	**b)** 100
_____ **3.** 22 + 19 + 9	**c)** 700
_____ **4.** 189 − 93	**d)** 90
_____ **5.** 234 + 512	**e)** 60

ESTIMATION WITH CALCULATOR ADDITION AND SUBTRACTION

Practicing with estimation will help you with calculator use. Estimating an answer will help you:

- choose an operation when you're not sure what to do
- detect a keying error when you have calculated incorrectly

Write

A. In each problem below, substitute round numbers, and compute an approximate answer. Use your approximate answer as a clue and choose the correct answer from the choices given.

1. Joyce paid $10.00 for a hairbrush that cost $6.19, including tax. How much change should Joyce receive?
    Substitute $6.00 for $6.19.

    a) $1.19
    b) $3.81
    c) $5.79

2. Attendance figures for three basketball games were as follows: Thursday—3,894, Friday—2,179, and Saturday—1,946. How many tickets were sold for these three games?
    Substitute 4,000 for 3,894, 2,000 for 2,179, and 2,000 for 1,946.

    a) 6,849
    b) 7,139
    c) 8,019

3. Ernie cut off a piece of pipe measuring 39 inches from a longer piece originally measuring 87 inches. What is the length of the remaining piece of pipe?
    Substitute 40 for 39 and 90 for 87.

    a) 28 inches
    b) 38 inches
    c) 48 inches

4. Friday's dinner cost Jan $6.79 for lasagna, $2.89 for dessert, and $1.09 for coffee. Not counting tax, what was the cost of Jan's meal?
    Substitute $7.00 for $6.79, $3.00 for $2.89, and $1.00 for $1.09.

    a) $10.77
    b) $12.47
    c) $13.87

Mental Calculation

B. For each of the following problems, use your calculator to compute an exact answer. Then estimate an answer in your head or with pencil and paper as you did on page 21. Did you make any keying errors? See how close your estimate was.

1. Count the total calories in the following meal:

ham and cheese sandwich:	397 calories
one glass of whole milk:	207 calories
one piece of cherry pie:	288 calories

_____
exact

_____
estimate

Questions 2–3 are based on the following drawing.

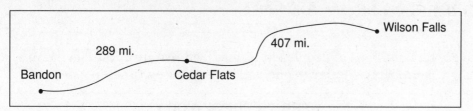

2. What is the distance between Bandon and Wilson Falls?

———————
exact

———————
estimate

3. How much farther is the distance from Cedar Flats to Wilson Falls than the distance from Cedar Flats to Bandon?

———————
exact

———————
estimate

Be careful. Questions 4–6 contain extra information—more information than you need to answer the questions.

4. At Sunday's sale, Jesse bought $23.88 worth of tools and an electric motor for $19.95. He also bought a small vise. After writing a check for $60.00, Jesse received $3.89 in change. How much did Jesse spend in all?

   Hint: Necessary information: $3.89, $60.00
       Extra information: $23.88, $19.95

———————
exact

———————
estimate

5. Of the 91 people entered in the Seniors' Jog-A-Thon, 19 are over 65 years of age, and only 29 are under 50 years of age. More than half, 49 to be exact, are women. Given these figures, determine the number of men entered in this year's Seniors' Jog-A-Thon.

———————
exact

———————
estimate

6. On the invoice shown at right, what is the total cost of the three newly purchased items, not counting the cost of the insurance, shipping, and C.O.D. service charges?

———————   ———————
exact   estimate

ANDERSON MANUFACTURING COMPANY			
Item #	**Description**	**Quantity**	**Amount**
28474B	Brass Table Lamp	1	$89.96
10277C	Oval Wall Mirror	1	$38.75
03278E	4-Shelf Bookcase	1	$48.89
	Returns		
89273A	3-Shelf Bookcase	1	($37.89)
	Insurance		$4.75
	Shipping		$13.85
	C.O.D. Service Charge		$3.00
		TOTAL COST	$161.31

ORDERING FROM A MENU

Every day, millions of people eat at fast food restaurants. The menu below is probably similar to one you've seen many times!

JERRY'S BURGER CITY

Sandwiches/Salads		Drinks		
Jerry's Single	$ .94	Soft Drinks	$.49,	$.79
Single Cheeseburger	1.09	Milk	.60,	.85
Jerry's Double	1.49	Coffee	.75,	.95
Double Cheeseburger	1.69	Tea	.50	
Chicken Sandwich	1.89	Hot Chocolate	.75	
Fish Sandwich	1.79			
Ham Sandwich	1.19	**Desserts**		
French Fries	$ .75, 1.25	Pie	$1.39	
		Cake	1.39	
Dinner Salad	1.49	Ice Cream	1.00	
Salad Bar	3.29			

Calculate

Use your calculator to help answer each question below. Use estimation to make sure your answer is sensible.

1. Robert is at Jerry's Burger City with his two children. He has only $7.00 to buy lunch for the three of them. Paying $.28 for tax, can he afford to buy the lunch listed at the right?

> 2 Single Cheeseburgers
> 1 Double Cheeseburger
> 2 Small French Fries
> 2 Small Milks
> 1 Large Coffee

2. After the game Saturday night, Danny and Gary stopped at Jerry's and ordered the food shown at right. Before taxes, how much will this meal cost them?

> 1 Double Cheeseburger
> 1 Chicken Sandwich
> 2 Large French Fries
> 1 Dinner Salad
> 2 Large Soft Drinks
> 2 Pieces of Pie

3. During her noon lunch break, Phyllis stopped by Jerry's for something to eat. She ordered a ham sandwich, a dinner salad, and a hot chocolate. How much was tax and tip if Phyllis spent a total of $4.05?

KEEPING A MILEAGE RECORD

People who use a car for work keep mileage records. Frank Barclay works as a truck driver for Lewiston Trucking Company. His partially completed weekly mileage record for the week of April 15 is shown below.

LEWISTON TRUCKING COMPANY
WEEKLY MILEAGE RECORD

Week Of: April 15   **Name:** Frank Barclay

	Date	Odometer Begins	Odometer Ends	Daily Mileage
Mon	4/15	38,643	39,025	382
Tue	4/16	39,025	39,432	
Wed	4/17	39,432	39,786	
Thu	4/18	39,786	40,216	
Fri	4/19	40,216	40,504	
Sat	4/20	40,504	40,880	
Sun	4/21	40,880	41,409	
			Weekly Total:	

To compute the daily mileage, subtract the reading under "Odometer Begins" from the reading under "Odometer Ends."

Example

Determine the number of miles Frank drove on Monday, April 15.

Odometer Ends	39,025
Odometer Begins	− 38,643
	382

Answer: **382 miles**

Calculate

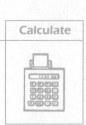

Use your calculator to help answer each question below.

1. Fill in the Daily Mileage column in the record above for Tuesday through Sunday.

2. Determine the total miles Frank drove during the week of April 15.

3. How many miles did Frank drive during the following time periods?

   a) During the weekend, Saturday and Sunday _____

   b) During the week, Monday through Friday _____

BALANCING A CHECKBOOK

Balancing a checkbook involves keeping a careful record of checking transactions: writing checks, making deposits, and paying bank service charges. A calculator can save you lots of time, especially if you need to recheck your work when your checkbook and bank statements don't match.

RECORDING TRANSACTIONS

Below is a sample **check register,** a page in a checkbook. The account holder, Leon Jenson, pays a bank service charge of $5.50 each month. He is not charged a fee for the checks that he writes.

RECORD ALL CHARGES OR CREDITS THAT AFFECT YOUR ACCOUNT

Number	Date	Description of Transaction	Payment/Debit (−)	✔ T	Fee (If Any) (−)	Deposit/Credit (+)	Balance $	
							568	43
202	6/1	North Street Apartments	$ 325 00	$	$		243	43
203	6/4	Amy's Market	29 74					
204	6/8	Import Auto Repair	109 66					
	6/15	Payroll Deposit				442 45		
205	6/19	Value Pharmacy	13 29					
206	6/21	Gazette Times	8 75					

REMEMBER TO RECORD AUTOMATIC PAYMENTS/DEPOSITS ON DATE AUTHORIZED

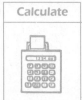

Calculate

1. Use your calculator to determine the daily balance of Leon's checking account. Record your answers in the BALANCE column of the register.
   - Subtract each check (PAYMENT/DEBIT column) from the BALANCE column.
   - Add each deposit (DEPOSIT/CREDIT column) to the BALANCE column.
2. Record the following new transactions in the register. Then compute Leon's daily balance up through June 30 and enter it on each line in the BALANCE column.
   Check 207, written to Nelsen's on June 23 for $39.83
   Check 208, written to Hi-Ho Foods on June 24 for $63.79
   Check 209, VOID (torn up)
   Check 210, written to Video Center on June 25 for $7.50
   Check reorder charge of $6.50 on June 26
   Payroll deposit of $442.45 on June 30
   Check 211, written to Washington Power on June 30 for $84.35

At the end of each month, the bank sends each customer a **bank statement.** A bank statement shows the checking account balance at the beginning and at the end of each month. It also shows deposits and checks that come back to the bank. Special bank service charges are also shown.

To **reconcile a bank statement** is to make sure it agrees with information on the check register.

The example bank statement below refers to Leon Jenson's check register shown on page 26.

Discovery

Many people like to check a calculation right after it's made. In a checkbook you can do this by

- *doing each addition or subtraction twice*

- *checking addition with subtraction, and checking subtraction with addition*

BANK STATEMENT

06/1 – 06/30	Beginning Balance	Deposits and Credits	Withdrawals and Debits	Ending Balance
Leon Jenson Checking Account	568.43	884.90	655.42	797.91

Monthly Service Charge		5.50
Check Reorder Charge	6/26	6.50

Checks

NBR	DATE	AMOUNT	NBR	DATE	AMOUNT
202	06/01	325.00	208	06/24	63.79
204*	06/08	109.66	210*	06/25	7.50
205	06/19	13.29	211	06/30	84.35
207*	06/23	39.83			

*Gap in check sequence
(This means that the check before it has not been cashed.)

Calculate

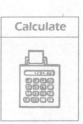

The exercise below shows you a step-by-step method to reconcile Leon's bank statement on this page with his check register on page 26.

Step 1. For each check that's listed on the bank statement on this page, place a check (✔) in the ✔ column of the check register.

Step 2. Add the amounts of the two June checks that Leon wrote which are not listed on the bank statement.

Step 3. Subtract the sum found in Step 2 from the June 30 Ending Balance reported on the bank statement.

Step 4. Subtract the bank service charge reported on the bank statement from the June 30 balance you wrote on the check register.

Step 5. Compare the amount computed in Step 3 to that computed in Step 4. Are they the same? If not, check your calculations for both the check register and for the steps of this exercise.

The ⓧ key is called the **multiply key** and is used to multiply two numbers.

Example 1

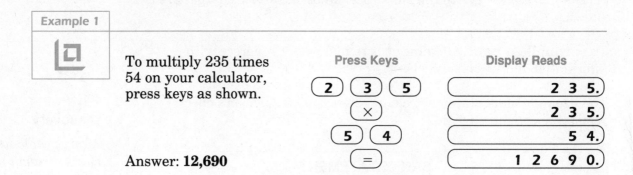

To multiply 235 times 54 on your calculator, press keys as shown.

Press Keys	Display Reads
2 3 5	2 3 5.
×	2 3 5.
5 4	5 4.
=	1 2 6 9 0.

Answer: **12,690**

As shown in Example 2, more than two numbers can be multiplied by pressing ⓧ before each new multiplication. As in addition and subtraction, you press ⓦ only once, after entering the final number to be multiplied.

Reminder: Clear your calculator display before you start a new problem.

Example 2

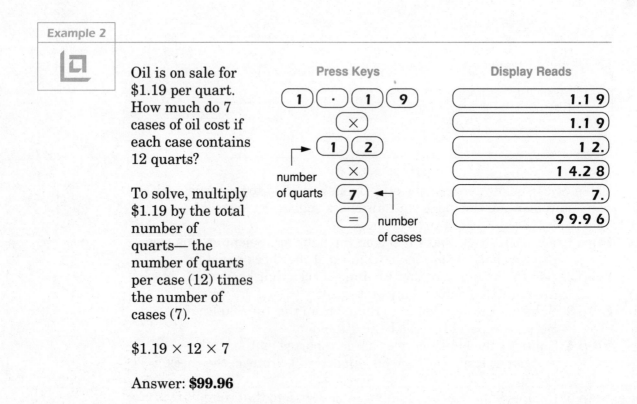

Oil is on sale for $1.19 per quart. How much do 7 cases of oil cost if each case contains 12 quarts?

To solve, multiply $1.19 by the total number of quarts— the number of quarts per case (12) times the number of cases (7).

$1.19 × 12 × 7

Answer: **$99.96**

Press Keys	Display Reads
1 · 1 9	1.1 9
×	1.1 9
1 2 (number of quarts)	1 2.
×	1 4.2 8
7 (number of cases)	7.
=	9 9.9 6

A. Fill in the numbers and the symbols to show how you would key in each problem. **Do not write the solution.**

1. the product of seventy-six and forty

⟨　⟩⟨　⟩⟨×⟩⟨　⟩⟨　⟩⟨=⟩

2. one hundred six times eighty-eight

⟨　⟩⟨　⟩⟨　⟩⟨　⟩⟨　⟩⟨　⟩

3. multiply nine dollars and four cents by seven

⟨　⟩⟨　⟩⟨　⟩⟨　⟩⟨　⟩⟨　⟩

Mental
Calculation

B. Compute both an exact answer and an estimate for each problem below. Remember that estimated answers can help you see if you have made keying errors.

- Round numbers between 10 and 100 to the nearest 10.

- Round numbers larger than 100 to the nearest 100.

	Exact	Estimate		Exact	Estimate		Exact	Estimate
1. a)	48	50	**b)**	67		**c)**	88	
	× 32	× 30		× 59			× 19	
		1,500						

	Exact	Estimate		Exact	Estimate		Exact	Estimate
2. a)	192	200	**b)**	289		**c)**	206	
	× 57	× 60		× 32			× 74	
		12,000						

Calculate

C. Solve each of the following problems on your calculator.

1. 7 × 8 × 5 =　　　19 × 8 × 6 =　　　23 × 17 × 5 =

2. 74 × 28 × 3 =　　　143 × 7 × 2 =　　　258 × 127 × 3 =

3. \$23.45 × 6 =　　　\$12.74 × 20 =　　　\$52.09 × 18 =

4. At the Labor Day sale, how much will Brad pay for 4 cases of orange juice concentrate?

Labor Day Special

Orange Juice
Concentrate

\$.89 per can

1 case

24 cans

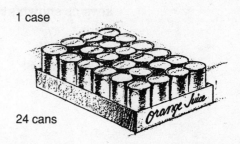

To divide is to see how many times one number (called the **divisor**) can go into a second number (called the **dividend**). The answer to a division problem is called the **quotient**.

As a quick review, the two ways that division problems are usually written are shown below.

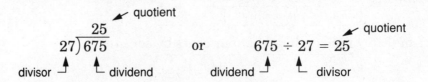

To divide on your calculator, follow these steps:

Step 1. Enter the dividend.

Step 2. Press $\div$, the divide key.

Step 3. Enter the divisor.

Step 4. Press $=$.

Example 1

$49\overline{)833}$

To solve, press keys as shown at right.

Answer: **17**

Press Keys	Display Reads
8 3 3	8 3 3.
÷	8 3 3.
4 9	4 9.
=	1 7.

Reminder: Clear your calculator display before you start a new problem.

Example 2

$\$39.76 \div 7$

To solve, press keys as shown at right.

Answer: **$5.68**

Press Keys	Display Reads
3 9 . 7 6	3 9.7 6
÷	3 9.7 6
7	7.
=	5.6 8

A. Identify the dividend and divisor in each problem below. Then fill in the key symbols to show how you would key in each problem on your calculator. **Do not write the answers.**

1. $19\overline{)152}$ dividend _____
                           divisor _____

2. $\$19.68 \div 8$ dividend _____
                           divisor _____

○○○○○○○   ○○○○○○○○

B. Using your calculator, compute an exact answer to each problem below. Then estimate an answer. Remember, estimated answers can help you see if you have made keying errors.

For the estimates in row 1, round each number to the nearest 10 before dividing.

Exact	Exact	Exact
1. $143 \div 11 =$	$153 \div 9 =$	$187 \div 11 =$

Estimate	Estimate	Estimate
$140 \div 10 = 14$		

For the estimates in row 2, round the dividend to the nearest 100 and the divisor to the nearest 10 before dividing.

Exact	Exact	Exact
2. $418 \div 19 =$	$693 \div 21 =$	$288 \div 18 =$

Estimate	Estimate	Estimate
$400 \div 20 = 20$		

C. Solve each of the following problems on your calculator.

1. $11\overline{)495}$ $14\overline{)364}$ $19\overline{)\$912}$ $28\overline{)\$1,708}$

2. Two hundred fifty-six people plan to attend this year's church picnic. If one table can seat 8, how many tables will be needed in all?

3. Mrs. Owens gives 56 music lessons each week. For these lessons she is paid a weekly total of $462. Determine how much Mrs. Owens charges for each lesson.

USING MATH "COMMON SENSE" WITH MULTIPLICATION AND DIVISION

Mental Calculation

A. Read the problems and use your "math common sense" to choose the correct answer. It's not necessary to do a computation.

1. If he takes home an average of $18 in tips each day, how many working days will it take Phil to save $558 from tips?

   a) multiplication: 10,044
   b) division: 31

2. There are 16 cups in one gallon. If a cup can hold eight ounces of liquid, how many ounces can a gallon hold?

   a) multiplication: 128
   b) division: 2

3. When cherries are on sale for $.84 per pound, how much do seven pounds of cherries cost?

   a) multiplication: $5.88
   b) division: $.12

4. If Frank types at the rate of 55 words per minute, how many minutes will it take him to type a report containing 1,760 words?

   a) multiplication: 96,800
   b) division: 32

Discovery

On some word problems, you may not know whether to multiply or divide. Do both on your calculator! As you see in part A, only one of the two answers will make sense.

Calculate

B. Estimate answers for problems 1–4. Use your calculator to compute the exact answers.

1. Last week, Joni worked a total of 39 hours. If her hourly pay rate is $4.89, how much were Joni's earnings last week before taxes?

   _____ estimate

   _____ exact

2. The Oregon state lottery prize of $1,972,800 is to be split equally among 9 winners. Determine each winner's share.

   _____ estimate

   _____ exact

3. West Side Tool Manufacturing makes and ships 3,914 wrenches each day. If a full shipping box contains 19 wrenches, how many boxes are needed each day by West Side Tool?

_____
estimate

_____
exact

4. The professional wrestling match between The Slippery Savage and Pretty Boy MacDougal attracted 7,090 fans. Each paid $4.75 for a ticket. What amount of money was brought in from ticket sales for this match?

_____
estimate

_____
exact

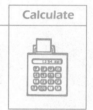

Calculate

C. Questions 1 through 4 refer to the following story. Each question requires its own specific information. This information may be entirely in the story, or it may be partly in the question itself. Choose information carefully as you answer each question.

Maria works as a secretary at Jackson Bookkeeping Services. For her work she receives $274 each week. Only two years ago, though, Maria worked as a maid at Starlight Motel and earned $168 each week.

Maria's husband, Mel, earns $14,508 each year as a lab technician at Lewis Electronic Fabricators.

1. When Maria worked as a maid, how much could she earn in one year if she worked all 52 weeks?

2. In her job as a secretary, how much does Maria now earn each year? (Maria is paid for 52 weeks of work even though she takes a two-week vacation.)

3. Assuming she works 40 hours each week, what is Maria paid hourly as a secretary?

4. Determine Mel's average weekly pay. Assume he is paid for 52 weeks.

Solving some problems involves more than one step.

Example

Ellen is buying 6 bottles of hair conditioner on sale. Each bottle costs $2.89. How much change will Ellen receive if she pays the clerk with a $20.00 bill?

Solving the example problem takes two steps: multiplication and subtraction.

Step 1. Multiply to find the cost of the conditioner:
$2.89 × 6 = $17.34

Step 2. Subtract the cost of the conditioner from $20.00:
$20.00 − $17.34 = $2.66

There are two methods for using a calculator to solve a multistep problem.

- **Method I:** Use pencil and paper to keep track of each step.

  Step 1: Multiply to find the cost of the conditioner. Then write the cost, $17.34, on paper so you don't forget it.

  Step 2: Clear the display and enter $20.00. Subtract $17.34 from $20.00 to get the answer $2.66.

- **Method II:** Use **memory keys** to keep track of each step. Pencil and paper are not needed. The discussion of memory keys begins on page 98.

Calculate

Use Method I to solve each of the following multistep problems.

1. At the Friday Halloween Sale, Judy bought three skirts on sale for $14.89 each. If she gave the clerk $50.00, how much change should Judy be given?

Hint:

cost of skirts = _____

change = _____

2. Linda cooks at Mom's Breakfasts restaurant. Last week she used 1,728 eggs. How many cases of eggs did she use if each case contains 24 cartons and each carton contains 12 eggs?

Hint:

number of eggs in each case = _____

number of cases used = _____

3. In the *News Tribune*, a weekend classified ad costs $5.75 for the first 16 words. Additional words are charged at the rate of $.23 per word. At this rate, how much will Randi pay for a 24-word ad?

Discovery

When adding a list of numbers, you may make a mistake on one entry. If you do, clear the display to erase this single number. Then, reenter the number correctly, and continue adding. In this way, ***you do not need to redo the whole problem.***

4. The brochure at the right lists the child care charges at the Little Bunnies Center. Li leaves her daughter at the center three full days each week and two half days. What amount is Li charged each week for child care?

LITTLE BUNNIES CENTER

Child Care Rates

Full Day	$14.75
Half Day	$ 8.25
Hourly	$ 2.50

5. Bea makes and sells flower baskets. Out of a total of 405 flowers, she plans to use 119 for large displays. The remaining flowers will be divided equally among 26 small flower baskets. How many flowers will be in each of these small flower baskets?

6. As assistant manager of Burger Supreme, Adah keeps track of weekly sales figures. The figures for the week of March 3 are shown at right. By how much is this week's total below Burger Supreme's weekly average of $15,283.28?

3/3 WEEKLY SALES FIGURES

Monday	$1,472.25
Tuesday	$1,784.04
Wednesday	$1,800.34
Thursday	$2,028.50
Friday	$2,135.79
Saturday	$2,465.93
Sunday	$2,233.34
Total:	

COMPLETING A PURCHASE ORDER

A **purchase order** (also called a **supply order**) is a form that a company fills out when it orders products from another company. Tina Vinson works for Downtown Hardware. Part of her job responsibility is to order items for the store as supplies run low. Her partially completed purchase order to Western Industrial Supply is shown below.

WESTERN INDUSTRIAL SUPPLY

	Item #	Description	Quantity	Cost/Per	Total Amount
1.	29-75A	Ace Cordless Drill	12	$12.45	# 149.40
2.	34-08V	3-Drawer Tool Chest	5	$39.99	
3.	03-14A	Star Claw Hammer	9	$ 6.95	
4.	07-24C	Delux Square Shovel	17	$ 8.88	
5.	47-83B	Bench-Grip Vise	8	$15.49	
6.	62-80B	10-Foot Ladder	6	$16.29	
7.	09-12A	#6 Screwdriver Set	16	$ 9.65	

Purchaser: *Tina Vinson* | **Total Purchase** |

To compute each Total Amount, multiply the Cost/Per times the Quantity. The Cost/Per is the price for each single described item.

Example

Determine the amount that Downtown Hardware must pay for 12 Ace Cordless Drills.

$$\begin{array}{r} \text{cost/per} \quad \$12.45 \\ \times \text{quantity} \quad \times 12 \\ \hline \text{total amount} \quad \$149.40 \end{array}$$

Answer: **$149.40**

Remember, your calculator will display ⟨ 1 4 9 . 4 ⟩ for $149.40. It does not show a 0 at the right-hand end of a decimal answer.

Calculate

Use your calculator to help answer each question below.

1. Complete the Total Amount column above for items 2 through 7.

2. Compute the Total Purchase by adding the seven entries in the Total Amount column.

3. When the order arrived, there was a note saying that Western Industrial no longer carried Star Claw Hammers. Since these hammers weren't shipped, what is the new Total Purchase amount?

DEPOSITING MONEY IN A CHECKING ACCOUNT

Retail businesses (those which sell directly to the public) take in money and checks every day. Accurately counting these receipts and depositing them in the company checking account is an important employee responsibility. Needless to say, a calculator can be a big help in a job like this.

The following definitions are used on a **checking account deposit slip:**
- **Currency:** paper money such as one-dollar bills, five-dollar bills, etc.
- **Coin:** coin money such as pennies, nickels, dimes, etc.
- **Cash Received:** money that you request the bank to give back to you from your deposit
- **Net Deposit:** the amount you actually deposit—the TOTAL minus CASH RECEIVED

FOR DEPOSIT TO THE ACCOUNT OF

SALLY'S ICE CREAMERY
4123 Colorado Blvd.
Denver, Colorado

DATE _____ 19 _____
DEPOSITS MAY NOT BE AVAILABLE FOR IMMEDIATE WITHDRAWAL

SIGN HERE FOR LESS CASH IN TELLER'S PRESENCE

NEW   DENVER OFFICE
HOPE   197 West Avenue
BANK   Denver, Colorado

CASH	CURRENCY	
	COIN	
LIST CHECKS SINGLY		
TOTAL FROM OTHER SIDE		
TOTAL		
LESS CASH RECEIVED		
NET DEPOSIT		

036

24-7938/3239

USE OTHER SIDE FOR
ADDITIONAL LISTING

*BE SURE EACH ITEM IS
PROPERLY ENDORSED*

CHECKS AND OTHER ITEMS ARE RECEIVED SUBJECT TO THE PROVISIONS OF THE UNIFORM COMMERCIAL CODE OR ANY APPLICABLE COLLECTIONS AGREEMENT.

Calculate

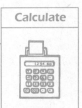

Each Tuesday morning, Brett deposits the business receipts of Sally's Ice Creamery. Today's deposit consists of the money indicated below.

Coins	Currency	Checks	
85 pennies	168 one-dollar bills	#24-72	$4.89
62 nickels	37 five-dollar bills	#31-29	$9.85
112 dimes	9 ten-dollar bills	#42-16	$20.00
247 quarters	3 twenty-dollar bills		

Use your calculator and write each of the following on the deposit slip:
1. the total amount of CURRENCY
2. the total amount of COIN
3. the amount of each CHECK
4. the TOTAL (CURRENCY, COIN, and CHECKS)—also write this TOTAL in the space labeled NET DEPOSIT

"BEST BUY" SHOPPING

Each time you make a purchase, you are faced with the question, "Which brand shall I buy?" Sometimes you prefer one brand over another, even if it costs more. Other times, you simply want the lowest price.

UNIT PRICING

Unit price is the amount you pay per single unit of purchase.
- If you're buying tomatoes by the pound, unit price is the price of each pound.
- If you're buying a dozen envelopes, unit price is the price of each envelope.

When the brand name is not important, you find the "best buy" by computing the lowest unit price:
- To compute unit price, divide the total price by the number of units purchased.

Example

Which of the following choices offers the best buy on peaches?

a) 6 lbs. for $3.84
b) 5 lb. bag for $2.95
c) 10 lb. bag for $.63 per lb.

To find the price per pound, divide the total price by the number of pounds.

a) $3.84 ÷ 6 = $.64   **b)** $2.95 ÷ 5 = $.59   **c)** Given as $.63 per lb.

Answer: Choice **b**, at **$.59 per pound** for a **5-pound bag,** is the best buy.

Calculate

Using your calculator, compute the unit price of each item below. Circle the best buy in each group.

1. orange juice concentrate
  a) $1.08 for 12 oz.
  b) $1.92 for 24 oz.
  c) $3.20 for 32 oz.

2. rolls of film
  a) 12-exposures for $2.88
  b) 24-exposures for $6.00
  c) 36-exposures for $8.28

3. multivitamins
  a) 75 tablets for $5.25
  b) 100 tablets for $8.00
  c) 150 tablets for $13.50

Total cost is the cost of purchasing several units of an item. To find the total cost:
- multiply unit price × number of items

For example, to buy 3 picture frames at $6.98:
$6.98 × 3 = $20.94

For some purchases, though, many stores give a discount when you buy several of the same item. For these purchases, finding the best buy involves taking advantage of discounts.

Example

When Smell Fresh dish soap went on sale at several stores, Patti decided to buy a case of 12 bottles. Which of the three stores below is offering the best buy?

Freddy's	**Home Foods**	**Value Foods**
Smell Fresh	Smell Fresh	Smell Fresh
Dish Soap	Dish Soap	Dish Soap
$1.19 per bottle	$1.29 per bottle	$1.29 per bottle
(no case discount)	$1.50 rebate	$.15 per bottle discount on
	each case	purchase of 12 or more

To find the best buy, compute the price of 12 bottles at each store.

Freddy's	**Home Foods**	**Value Foods**
$1.19 × 12 = $14.28	($1.29 × 12) − $1.50	$1.29 − .15 = $1.14
		$1.14 × 12 = $13.68
	= $15.48 − $1.50	
	= $13.98	

Answer: **Value Foods** is offering the best buy at $13.68.

Calculate

Circle the store in each group that is offering the best buy.

1. 15 pounds of oranges

Freddy's: $.98 per pound

Home Foods: $.99 per pound, $.50 discount on 15-lb. bag

Value Foods: $1.09 per pound, $1.50 rebate for purchases of $10.00 or more

2. 12 quarts of Super Deluxe car oil

Save More: $1.04 per quart

Buy Right: $1.19 per quart, $1.00 discount on case of 12

Henry's: $1.13 per quart, "Buy 11 and get 1 free!"

COMPUTING DISTANCE, RATE, AND TIME

Just think how often you've asked these questions:

How far is it? How fast are we going? How long will it take?

These three quantities—distance, rate, and time—are related by the
distance formula: Distance equals Rate times Time.

Distance (D)	**=**	**Rate (R)**	**×**	**Time (T)**
Usually expressed in miles		Speed—usually expressed in miles per hour (mph)		Usually expressed in hours

Written in short form as $D = RT$, the distance formula is used to find
the distance when the rate and time are known. Once again, using a
calculator carefully can be a big help.

Example 1

The bus between Chicago and New York averages 45 miles per hour.
How far can this bus travel in the first 8 hours of the trip?
Step 1. Identify R and T.
    $R = 45$ miles per hour $T = 8$ hours
Step 2. Substitute the R and T values into the distance formula and
multiply.
    $D = RT = 45 \times 8 =$ **360 miles**

The distance formula can also be expressed as a **rate formula** (the
speed) or **time formula.**

| Rate Formula: $R = D \div T$ | | Time Formula: $T = D \div R$ |

Example 2

On Sunday, Ann drove 336 miles in 8 hours. What average speed did
Ann drive?
Step 1. Identify D and T.
    $D = 336$ miles $T = 8$ hours
Step 2. Substitute the D and T values into the rate formula.
    $R = D \div T = 336 \div 8 =$ **42 mph**

Example 3

How long will it take Alex to complete the 105-mile bicycle race if he
averages 15 miles per hour?
Step 1. Identify D and R.
    $D = 105$ miles $R = 15$ mph
Step 2. Substitute the D and R values into the time formula.
    $T = D \div R = 105 \div 15 =$ **7 hours**

In each problem, decide whether you are trying to find the **distance, rate,** or **time.** Then, using the correct formula, calculate your answer.

Distance Formula: $D=RT$	Rate Formula: $R=D \div T$	Time Formula: $T=D \div R$

1. Over a two-day period, Dale rode a total of 14 hours on a bike ride from Portland to Seattle. If he rode a total distance of 182 miles, what average speed did he ride?

2. On the first day of her trip to Canada, June averaged 49 miles per hour for seven straight hours. What distance did June drive during this time?

3. Averaging 620 miles per hour, how long will it take an airliner to travel across the United States, a distance of 3,255 miles?

4. If he stays within the speed limit of 65 miles per hour, what is the farthest that Owen can drive in 9 hours on the road?

5. Last Saturday, Pam was travelling for a total of 13 hours. Except for the hour she stopped for lunch and the hour for dinner, she was driving. If she drove a total of 572 miles, what was Pam's average driving speed?

> Ask yourself, "How many hours did Pam actually drive?"

6. Brandon left home at 8:00 A.M. Tuesday. If he drove at the speed limit of 55 mph all the way, at what time did he arrive in Chicago, a distance of 275 miles from his home?

> First, figure out how many hours Brandon drove.

7. What speed must Erik average if he leaves home at 1:00 P.M. and hopes to reach San Francisco by 6:00 P.M., a distance of 265 miles away?

> How many hours does Erik want to drive?

Remainders in Division

Many division problems contain a remainder as part of
the answer. For example, if you divide 17 sheets of
drawing paper among five students, each student gets 3
sheets. Since 5×3 is 15, 2 sheets are left over. Dividing
17 by 5 gives an answer of 3 with a remainder of 2.

$$\begin{array}{r} 3\text{ r }2 \\ 5\overline{)17} \\ 15 \\ \hline 2 \end{array}$$

Mathematically, there are three ways to write a remainder:
- As a whole number following the letter r
- As the numerator (top number) of a fraction in which the
  denominator (bottom number) is the divisor
- As a decimal fraction. A decimal point is added to the right of the
  whole number part of the answer, and the division is carried out
  beyond the decimal point.

The remainder in our example, $17 \div 5$, can be written in each of these
three ways:

a) as a whole number
following r

$$\begin{array}{r} 3\text{ r }2 \\ 5\overline{)17} \\ 15 \\ \hline 2 \end{array}$$

b) as the numerator of
a fraction

$$\begin{array}{r} 3\frac{2}{5} \\ 5\overline{)17} \\ 15 \\ \hline 2 \end{array}$$

c) as a decimal
fraction

$$\begin{array}{r} 3.4 \\ 5\overline{)17.0} \\ 15 \\ \hline 2\,0 \\ 2\,0 \end{array}$$

Calculator Division

As you may have already discovered, your calculator displays a
remainder as a decimal fraction. We'll work with decimal fractions on
page 48. On this page and the next, you'll see interesting types of
problems you can already do.

Example 1

Packing six books in each
box, how many boxes will
Lena need for 189 books?

To solve, divide 189 by 6.
The whole number part of
the answer tells us that 31
boxes will contain exactly six books. One more
box will be needed to pack the remainder.

Answer: **32 boxes** $(31 + 1)$

Press Keys	Display Reads
1 8 9	1 8 9.
÷	1 8 9.
6	6.
=	3 1 . 5

31 boxes

1 more box is
needed to
pack remaining
books

Example 2

José and two friends agreed to split the cost of a large pizza. If the pizza cost $14.30, what was José's share?

To solve, divide $14.30 by 3. Press keys as shown at right.

Press Keys

(1)(4)(·)(3)(0)

(÷)

Display Reads

(1 4.3 0)

(1 4.3 0)

Write the displayed answer to the nearest cent.

(3)

(÷)

(3.)

(=)

(4.7 6 6 6 6 6 6)

cents

Answer: **$4.77**

Note: When you write to the nearest cent, ask yourself, "What is this closest to?" Is Example 2 closer to $4.76 or $4.77? It is closer to $4.77.

Calculate

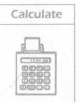

A. Solve each division problem below. Identify both the whole number part of the answer and the remainder.

	Displayed Answer	Whole Number Part	Remainder
1. $126 \div 8 =$	15.75	15	.75
2. $171 \div 4 =$			
3. $208 \div 5 =$			
4. $293 \div 8 =$			
5. $356 \div 3 =$			

B. Solve each word problem below. Be sure to consider the remainder in your answer.

1. Erwin can haul 12 cubic yards of dirt in a single truckload. How many trips will Erwin need to make in order to move 203 cubic yards of dirt from the construction site?

2. Sammy and two friends are splitting the cost of lunch. If the total meal plus tax comes to $17.87, what is Sammy's share to the nearest penny?

3. Part of Joe's job as a salesman is to set up display cases of the type of dolls that his company sells. If Joe can get a maximum of six dolls in each case, how many display cases will he need in order to display a total of 23 dolls?

In some problems, you want to know the value of a remainder.

Example 1

Jason must haul 94 cubic yards of dirt by the end of the day. His truck can carry a maximum of 12 cubic yards. Assuming he fills his truck when possible, how much dirt will Jason carry on his final load?

Dividing 94 by 12, you get:

$94 \div 12 = 7.8333333$

7 trips

1 trip with a partial load

This means that Jason will make 7 trips, each with a full load of 12 cubic yards, and 1 final trip with a partial load.

How Large is the Remainder?

Now Jason wants to know how many cubic yards of dirt he will carry in the partial load.

Step 1. Find the amount of dirt hauled in full loads.

7 × 1 2 = 8 4. cubic yards

Step 2. Subtract to find the amount of dirt in the partial load.

9 4 − 8 4 = 1 0. cubic yards

Example 2

Divide 1,293 by 172. Write the value of the remainder.

Step 1. Divide 1,293 by 172.

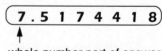

7 . 5 1 7 4 4 1 8

whole number part of answer

Step 2. Multiply using the whole number part of the answer.
$7 \times 172 = 1,204$

Step 3. Subtract to find the value of the remainder.
$1,293 - 1,204 = 89$

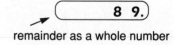

8 9.

remainder as a whole number

Answer: **7 r 89**

A. Complete the steps in the following problem.

Find the whole number remainder in 598 ÷ 27.

Step 1. Divide 598 by 27.
Displayed answer: _____

Step 2. Multiply the whole number part of the answer found in
Step 1 by 27.
Displayed answer: _____

Step 3. Subtract the answer found in Step 2 from 598.
Displayed answer: _____

Whole number remainder = _____

B. Divide with your calculator and write each answer with a whole
number remainder.

1. 258 ÷ 17 = _____ r _____   **3.** 749 ÷ 41 = _____ r _____

2. 494 ÷ 53 = _____ r _____   **4.** 980 ÷ 25 = _____ r _____

C. Solve each word problem below.

1. On another job, Jason agreed
to remove 114 cubic yards of
gravel from a building site.
Assuming he again carries 12
cubic yards each full load,
how much gravel will Jason
carry on his final load?

2. On her cross-country trip,
Shari drove 350 miles each
day except her final day. If
she drove a total of 3,185
miles, determine the number
of miles Shari drove the
final day of the trip.

Discovery

*Once in a while, you may accidentally try to do a calculation that
your calculator is unable to do. The calculator will then display an
error symbol—an* E *on most calculators. Here are two examples.*

- **Overflow error:** *Multiplying numbers that
give a product that is too large for the display.
Example: 18,500 × 9,650*

  $$\boxed{1 . 7 8 5 2 5 0 0 \text{OE}}$$

- **Division by 0 error:** *Trying to
divide by 0. You cannot divide by 0.
Example: 45 ÷ 0*

  $$\boxed{0.\text{E}}$$

If an error symbol appears on your calculator, simply press a
clear *key and redo your calculation.*

PUZZLE POWER

By now you're probably pretty good at using a calculator. Review your skills by working these problems. Write your answers in the puzzle.

Across

1. 37×19

3. the number of cents more than $6.00 in the amount $6.20

4. $451 + 396 + 84$

6. $36.27 rounded to the nearest $10.00

7. the best estimate of the product 39×21: 700, 800, or 900

9. $30.25 \times 4 \times 3$

10. the whole number part of the quotient $143 \div 14$

Down

1. $4{,}284 \div 6$

2. $702 \div 18$

3. $20.87 rounded to the nearest dollar

5. $1{,}241 - 529 - 362$

7. 827 rounded to the nearest 10

8. the digits displayed when you enter $.19 on your calculator

9. the best estimate of the quotient $892 \div 31$: 30, 40, or 50

PART 3

Decimals and Fractions

Working with decimals comes easily on a calculator. Most people already do some of this when they use a calculator to work problems involving money. Fractions are a little trickier to work out on a calculator, but you'll learn an easy way to work with them.

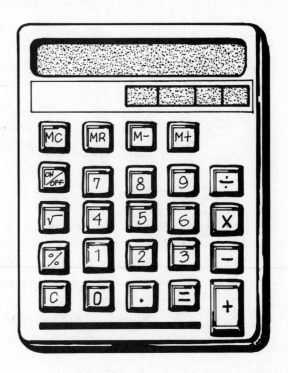

What's the most common use of decimal fractions? You're correct if you answer, "Money!"

- Cents are the **decimal fraction** part of a dollar.

Your calculator shows the second most common use of decimal fractions:

- They express a **remainder** in a division problem.

Reading Decimals

To get yourself ready to work with decimal place value, review the meaning of each simple decimal fraction below.

Decimal	Value	Meaning
.1	one tenth	1 part out of 10 parts
.01	one hundredth	1 part out of 100 parts
.001	one thousandth	1 part out of 1,000 parts
.0001	one ten-thousandth	1 part out of 10,000 parts
.00001	one hundred-thousandth	1 part out of 100,000 parts
.000001	one millionth	1 part out of 1,000,000 parts

Example

Read the decimal .042.

Step 1. Read the number to the right of the decimal point.

.042 reads as 42

Step 2. Read the place value of the digit farthest to the right.

.042
↑ thousandths

Step 3. Put the number and the place value name together.

.042 is **42 thousandths**

Mixed Decimals

A **mixed decimal** is a whole number plus a decimal fraction. The number 7.18 is a mixed decimal. So is the amount $3.99.

mixed decimal = whole number + decimal fraction

When reading a mixed decimal, read the decimal point as the word *and*.

For example, 7.18 is read "7 *and* 18 hundredths." The money amount $3.99 is read "3 dollars *and* 99 cents."

A. Write words to express the value of each decimal fraction below.

1. .05 _____

4. .005 _____

2. .5 _____

5. .00005 _____

3. .000005 _____

6. .0005 _____

B. Determine the value of each displayed number below. Choose each answer from the choices given.

1. ⎛ 0 . 2 0 6 ⎞
  a) 26 hundredths
  b) 206 hundredths
  c) 206 thousandths

4. ⎛ 0 . 1 5 ⎞
  a) 15 hundredths
  b) 15 thousandths
  c) 150 ten-thousandths

2. ⎛ 0 . 0 4 7 ⎞
  a) 47 tenths
  b) 47 hundredths
  c) 47 thousandths

5. ⎛ 0 . 0 0 9 ⎞
  a) 9 tenths
  b) 9 thousandths
  c) 9 ten-thousandths

3. ⎛ 0 . 7 ⎞
  a) 7 tenths
  b) 7 hundredths
  c) 7 thousandths

6. ⎛ 0 . 0 8 ⎞
  a) 8 tenths
  b) 8 hundredths
  c) 80 hundredths

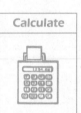

C. Use your calculator to solve each of the following division problems. Choose the correct answer from the choices given.

1. 1 ÷ 8 =
  a) 1 and 25 tenths
  b) 125 thousandths
  c) 1 and 25 hundredths

4. 5 ÷ 16 =
  a) 3,125 hundredths
  b) 3,125 thousandths
  c) 3,125 ten-thousandths

2. 9 ÷ 100 =
  a) 9 tenths
  b) 9 hundredths
  c) 9 thousandths

5. 20 ÷ 80 =
  a) 25 tenths
  b) 2 and 5 tenths
  c) 25 hundredths

3. 30 ÷ 8 =
  a) 375 hundredths
  b) 3 and 75 hundredths
  c) 3 and 75 thousandths

6. 245 ÷ 56 =
  a) 4 and 375 thousandths
  b) 4,375 ten-thousandths
  c) 4,375

For most problems, you will only need one or two decimal places.

Example

Gasoline prices are always given to three decimal places. If the price per gallon is $1.189, how much do 16 gallons of gas cost?

$1.189 × 16 = $19.024
This answer rounds to $19.02.

In many cases, a rounded answer will do. You can use the sign ≈ to mean "is approximately equal to."

$1.189 × 16 = $19.024 ≈ **$19.02**

Rounding a Decimal Fraction

Steps for rounding decimal fractions:

Step 1. Underline the digit in the decimal place you wish to round to.

Step 2. Look at the digit to the right of the underlined digit.

- If the digit to the right is 5 or more, add 1 to the underlined digit.

- If the digit to the right is less than 5, leave the underlined digit as it is.

- Discard all digits to the right of the underlined digit.

Numbers rounded to 10ths place

tenths place

0.3̲82 ≈ 0.4

5 or more,
so 0.382 rounds to 0.4

tenths place

4.6̲3 ≈ 4.6

less than 5,
so 4.63 rounds to 4.6

Numbers rounded to 100ths place

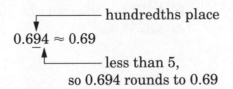

hundredths place

0.69̲4 ≈ 0.69

less than 5,
so 0.694 rounds to 0.69

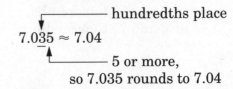

hundredths place

7.03̲5 ≈ 7.04

5 or more,
so 7.035 rounds to 7.04

A. Round each amount below to the nearest 10¢. Circle one of the two answer choices.

1. $0.27: $0.20 or $(\$0.30)$ **4. $0.62:** $0.60 or $0.70

2. $0.95: $0.90 or $1.00   **5. $3.55:** $3.50 or $3.60

3. $7.93: $7.90 or $8.00   **6. $4.05:** $4.00 or $4.10

B. Round each number below to the place value indicated.

	10ths	100ths			100ths	1,000ths
1. 3.457	3.5	3.46	**5.**	8.0073	8.01	8.007
2. 14.382	___	___	**6.**	24.0049	___	___
3. 38.945	___	___	**7.**	90.8307	___	___
4. 40.050	___	___	**8.**	72.3846	___	___

C. Divide with your calculator. Write both the displayed answer and the rounded answer.

In row 1, round each answer to the 10ths place.
1. $16 \div 13 = 1.2307692$ $11 \div 8 =$ $24 \div 7 =$

≈ 1.2 ↑ less than 5 $\approx$ ___ $\approx$ ___

In row 2, round each answer to the 100ths place.
2. $\$31 \div 16 = \$1.9375$ $15 \div 8 =$ $\$17 \div 9 =$

$\approx \$1.94$ ↑ 5 or more $\approx$ ___ $\approx$ ___

In row 3, round each answer to the 1,000ths place.
3. $23 \div 16 = 1.4375$ $45 \div 22 =$ $16 \div 7 =$

≈ 1.438 ↑ 5 or more $\approx$ ___ $\approx$ ___

D. Solve each word problem below.

1. A jeweler wishes to cut a 33-inch long gold wire into 7 equal pieces. To the nearest 100th inch, how long should each of the 7 pieces be?

2. One inch equals 2.54 centimeters. How many centimeters are equal to the length of 1 yard (36 inches)? Express your answer to the nearest tenth centimeter.

TERMINATING AND REPEATING DECIMALS

Decimals result each time you:
  • divide one number by another and get a remainder

$$(6) ÷ (4) (=) \boxed{1.5}$$

  • divide a smaller number by a larger number

$$(4) ÷ (6) (=) \boxed{0.6666666}$$

For each type of division, the decimal is said to be either **terminating** or **repeating.**

Terminating Decimals

A terminating decimal fraction has a limited number of digits. The answers to most decimal problems have four or fewer digits to the right of the decimal point.

Examples

One decimal
digit 3 ÷ 5 = .6

$$(3) ÷ (5) (=) \boxed{0.6}$$

Two decimal digits
7 ÷ 4 = 1.75

$$(7) ÷ (4) (=) \boxed{1.75}$$

Three decimal digits
21 ÷ 8 = 2.625

$$(2)(1) ÷ (8) (=) \boxed{2.625}$$

Repeating Decimals

A repeating decimal fraction has a never-ending, repeating pattern of one or more digits. Look at these examples:

Examples

Single repeating digit 4 ÷ 9 = .444 . . .

$$(4) ÷ (9) (=) \boxed{0.4444444}$$

Two repeating digits 144 ÷ 66 = 2.1818 . . .

$$(1)(4)(4) ÷ (6)(6) (=) \boxed{2.1818181}$$

Three repeating digits 148 ÷ 999 = .148148 . . .

$$(1)(4)(8) ÷ (9)(9)(9) (=) \boxed{0.1481481}$$

Notice that a repeating digit pattern continues forever! For this reason, a calculator gives an approximate answer to any division problem that results in a repeating decimal.

Try this division problem on your calculator: 2 ÷ 3 = _____

- If your answer is 0.6666666, your calculator **truncates** (drops) any digits that won't fit on your display.

- If your answer is 0.6666667, your calculator **rounds** the answer to the final decimal place on your calculator display.

Most likely, your calculator truncates. Almost all inexpensive calculators do. Expensive calculators—those designed for use in business and in science—round repeating decimals. See if anyone in your class has a rounding calculator.

Write

A. Using pencil and paper, perform each division below. Indicate with a check (✔) the type of decimal answer you obtain.

1. 4)5 _____ terminating
_____ repeating

3. 33)5 _____ terminating
_____ repeating

2. 3)1 _____ terminating
_____ repeating

4. 8)7 _____ terminating
_____ repeating

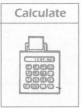

Calculate

B. Use your calculator to perform each division below. Below each problem, indicate the pattern of repeating digits. Problem 1 is completed as an example.

1. 17 ÷ 11 = 1.5454545

repeating digits: 0.54 . . .

3. 23 ÷ 9 =

repeating digits:

2. 4 ÷ 3 =

repeating digits:

4. 8 ÷ 33 =

repeating digits:

As you saw on pages 52 and 53, repeating digits form what is called a **pattern.** When you recognize a pattern, you can predict what will come next.

In your work with math, it will help to look for patterns. These next pages will give you practice with patterns, first in shapes, words, letters, and numbers, and then with word problems.

Write

A. See if you can draw the next shape in each pattern below.

1. , 3.

2. △, □, ⬠, ____ 4. |, ⌐, ⊓, ____

B. Try to finish these familiar word patterns.

1. ten, nine, _____ 3. small, smaller, _____

2. ready, set, _____ 4. eeny, meeny, miny, _____

C. What is the next number or letter in each series below?

1. 1, 3, 6, 10, 15, _____ 3. 6, 15, 7, 14, 8, _____

2. A, Z, B, Y, C, _____ 4. A, C, F, J, O, _____

Calculate

D. Use your calculator to do the first three problems in each column. Then, using the answer patterns as a guide, predict the answer to each starred (*) problem.

1. $1001 \times 46 =$
    $1001 \times 52 =$
    $1001 \times 28 =$
    $*1001 \times 34 =$
    $*1001 \times 16 =$

3. $37 \times 6 =$
    $37 \times 9 =$
    $37 \times 12 =$
    $*37 \times 15 =$
    $*37 \times 21 =$

2. $10 \div 9 =$
    $11 \div 9 =$
    $12 \div 9 =$
    $*13 \div 9 =$
    $*15 \div 9 =$

4. $12 \div 33 =$
    $13 \div 33 =$
    $14 \div 33 =$
    $*15 \div 33 =$
    $*17 \div 33 =$

E. Word problems also follow patterns. The most familiar patterns are listed below.

Some Word Problem Patterns	
Addition	sum or combined amount
Subtraction	how much larger one amount is or the difference between two amounts
Multiplication	given cost (or size) of one item, find the cost (or size) of many
Division	given the total cost (or size) of several items, find the cost (or size) of one

In each problem below, circle the symbol standing for the pattern you recognize. Then use your calculator to solve each problem.

1. Angie wants to save $510 to buy a new stereo. How much must she save per month if she plans to buy the stereo in one year's time? (one year = 12 months)

   Pattern: $+$ $-$ $\times$ $\div$ Answer: _____

2. When she bought her house, Karla paid $48,795. She recently sold this house for $17,980 more than she paid for it. Given these figures, determine the sale price of the house.

   Pattern: $+$ $-$ $\times$ $\div$ Answer: _____

3. When he started his diet, Lucas weighed 236 pounds. During the first 3 months, he lost 17 pounds. Now, six months later, Lucas weighs 199 pounds. How much has Lucas lost in all?

   Pattern: $+$ $-$ $\times$ $\div$ Answer: _____

4. Hanna's car gets 22 miles per gallon in city driving and 28 miles per gallon on the highway. How many miles of city driving can Hanna expect to do on each 16-gallon fill up?

   Pattern: $+$ $-$ $\times$ $\div$ Answer: _____

5. George and four friends are going camping. They've agreed that each of them should carry the same amount of weight while hiking. If the gear weighs 142 pounds, what weight should each of them carry?

   Pattern: $+$ $-$ $\times$ $\div$ Answer: _____

When you use paper and pencil to add, the first step is to line up decimal points. When you use a calculator, this step is done for you. You will be able to catch keying errors if you keep your eye on decimal places in the answers.

Example 1

To add 12.047 and 9.36 on your calculator, press the keys as shown.

Answer: **21.407**

Press Keys	Display Reads
(1)(2)(·)(0)(4)(7)	1 2 . 0 4 7
(+)	1 2 . 0 4 7
(9)(·)(3)(6)	9 . 3 6
(=)	2 1 . 4 0 7

Discovery

When you use paper and pencil to add and subtract decimal numbers, you may add a place-holding zero.

Pencil and Paper

```
  12.047
+  9.360 ←— place-
  21.407   holding 0
```

When you use a calculator, you do not have to enter place-holding 0's.

Example 2

To add $5.60, $9, and $7.82, press the keys as shown.

Answer: **$22.42**

Press Keys	Display Reads
(5)(·)(6)(0)	5 . 6
(+)	5 . 6
(9)	9 .
(+)	1 4 . 6
(7)(·)(8)(2)	7 . 8 2
(=)	2 2 . 4 2

Discovery

When you add a whole number to a decimal number, you do not need to enter a decimal point to the right of the whole number. The calculator does this for you.

A. Practice keeping your eye on decimal places so you can catch "keying errors." Complete each problem below by placing a decimal point in the answer. If you find it helpful, rewrite each problem in a column (up and down).

1. .56 + .8 = 1 3 6   .7 + .29 = 9 9   2.4 + .75 + .8 = 3 9 5

2. .07 + .09 = 1 6   1.6 + .9 = 2 5   3.06 + 8 + .59 = 1 1 6 5

B. Calculate an exact answer to each problem below. Then compute an estimate, following these guidelines:
  • Round numbers smaller than 10 to the nearest whole number.
  • Round numbers between 10 and 99 to the nearest 10.
  • Round numbers equal to 100 or more to the nearest 100.

	Exact	Estimate		Exact	Estimate		Exact	Estimate
1. a)	8.3	8	**b)**	9.7		**c)**	6.3	
	+ 5.6	+ 6		+ 6.5			+ 7.1	
	13.9	14						

	Exact	Estimate		Exact	Estimate		Exact	Estimate
2. a)	25.8	30	**b)**	75.60		**c)**	27.85	
	+ 13.6	+ 10		+ 24.83			+ 12.4	
	39.4	40						

	Exact	Estimate		Exact	Estimate		Exact	Estimate
3. a)	328.65	300	**b)**	547.69		**c)**	900	
	211.06	200		243.63			375.8	
	+ 123	+ 100		+ 181.8			+ 245.18	
	662.71	600						

C. Calculate the exact answer to each problem. Round each answer to the nearest whole number (or dollar).

1. 21.8 + 14.7 =   57.14 + 37.5 = $154.85 + $49.50 =

2. 250 + 136.8 =   231.8 + 85.95 = $34.54 + $23.50 =

D. Find the combined length in inches of the three spacers pictured at right.

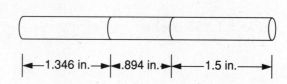

|←—1.346 in.—→|←.894 in.→|←—1.5 in.—→|

SUBTRACTING TWO OR MORE DECIMAL NUMBERS

You subtract decimal numbers in the same way you subtract whole numbers. Be sure to enter the larger number on the calculator first! In decimal subtraction, as in decimal addition, the calculator lines up decimal points for you.

Example 1

To subtract 4.76 from 9.1 on your calculator, press the keys as shown.

Press Keys	Display Reads
9 . 1	9.1
−	9.1
4 . 7 6	4.7 6
=	4.3 4

Answer: **4.34**

Example 2

To subtract 3.5 and 8.375 from 15, press the keys shown.

Press Keys	Display Reads
1 5	1 5.
−	1 5.
3 . 5	3.5
−	1 1.5
8 . 3 7 5	8.3 7 5
=	3.1 2 5

Answer: **3.125**

Example 3

Fran must cut a rod so that its finished diameter is 8.765 inches. If she starts with a 10-inch diameter rod, how much will Fran need to remove?

Press Keys	Display Reads
1 0	1 0.
−	1 0.
8 . 7 6 5	8.7 6 5
=	1.2 3 5

To solve, subtract 8.765 from 10.

Answer: **1.235 inches**

When you subtract decimal fractions, first decide which decimal is larger. (You will enter the larger decimal in the calculator first.)

Example 4

Sam Rogers is 1.46 meters tall, and his brother Ken is 1.7 meters tall. Which brother is taller and by how much?

Step 1. Compare the decimal places. If there are not the same number of places, add 0's to give them the same number of places.

1.7	1.46
1.70	1.46
larger	

Step 2. Subtract the smaller number from the larger.

$1.70 - 1.46 = .24$

Answer: **Ken Rogers is .24 meters taller.**

Write

A. Circle the larger decimal fraction in each pair below.

1. .81 or .79 **2.** .102 or .11 **3.** .035 or .0093

Calculate

B. Find the difference between each pair of decimal fractions below. (If you accidentally subtract the larger fraction from the smaller, your calculator will display a minus sign next to the answer.)

1. .36 and .59 .93 and .755 .405 and .386

2. .09 and .134 .8 and .79 .354 and .38

C. Calculate the answer to each problem.

1. .298
     − .145

2. $13.45
     − 8.80

3. $25 − 12.45 − 11.85

4. When she had the flu, Shannon's temperature rose as shown below. How much higher is her fever temperature than normal?

|← Normal human body temperature
98.6° F |← Shannon's temperature
                    104° F

Fahrenheit

92 96 98 100 2 4 6 8 10

Mental Calculation

A. In problems 1–3, substitute whole numbers for decimal numbers and estimate an answer. Using your estimate as a guide, choose the exact answer from the choices given. (Estimate, don't calculate!)

1. At a picnic, two tables were placed end to end. If the first table is 2.89 meters long and the second is 1.94 meters long, what is the combined length in meters of the two tables?

   (Substitute 3 for 2.89 and 2 for 1.94.)

   a) 3.13
   b) 4.83
   c) 6.73

2. Ming is trying to decide which of two pork roasts to buy. One weighs 4.79 pounds, and the other weighs 6.2 pounds. By how many pounds is the larger roast heavier than the smaller?

   (Substitute 5 for 4.79 and 6 for 6.2.)

   a) 1.41
   b) 2.61
   c) 3.01

3. Jason Sports is advertising that ski jacket prices have been "drastically reduced from $61.89 to $39.99." How much of a savings is this advertised price reduction?

   (Substitute $60 for $61.89 and $40 for $39.99.)

   a) $14.80
   b) $16.90
   c) $21.90

Calculate

B. For problems 1–3, use your calculator to compute an exact answer. Then estimate an answer as a check against keying errors.

1. With his football uniform on, Rocky can run the 100-yard dash in 14.26 seconds. Wearing only running clothes, he can run the same distance in 11.89 seconds. How much faster can Rocky run the 100-yard dash when he's not wearing football gear?

   ——————
   exact

   ——————
   estimate

2. Rose switched to super unleaded gas and found that her gas mileage went from 27.8 miles per gallon to 30.2 miles per gallon. By how many miles per gallon did the super unleaded gas improve her mileage?

———————
exact

———————
estimate

3. Following the weekend sale, The Gift Shoppe raised the prices of all vases by $2.29. What would be the new price of a vase that had been priced at $11.88 during the sale?

———————
exact

———————
estimate

For problems 4–6, look at the list or drawing to the right of each problem to find necessary information.

4. As shown on the map at the right, Leslie lives almost halfway between the theater and the swimming pool. By how many miles is Leslie closer to one than the other?

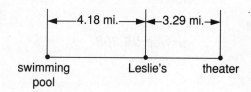

|←——4.18 mi.——→|←——3.29 mi.——→|

swimming
pool   Leslie's   theater

———————   ———————
exact   estimate

5. Gloria keeps a record of her gasoline purchases. Part of that record is shown at right. How many more gallons of gas did Gloria purchase on February 28 than on January 24?

Date	Gallons
1/9	21.4
1/24	18.9
2/11	17.9
2/28	20.7

———————   ———————
exact   estimate

6. Expressing your answer as a decimal fraction, how much longer is the longest bolt than the shortest bolt?

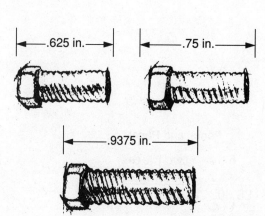

|←—.625 in.—→| |←——.75 in.——→|

|←———.9375 in.———→|

———————   ———————
exact   estimate

MULTIPLYING TWO OR MORE DECIMAL NUMBERS

You can use your calculator to multiply a decimal number times a whole number or to multiply two or more decimal numbers.

- As in whole number multiplication, enter each number into the calculator and press ⊗ . Press ⊜ only once, after the final number is multiplied.

Example 1

To multiply 6.84 times 3.7 on your calculator, press the keys as shown.

Answer: **25.308**

Press Keys	Display Reads
6 · 8 4	6.84
×	6.84
3 · 7	3.7
=	25.308

Example 2

Multiply: $5.06 \times 4 \times .088$. Round the answer to the nearest cent.

To solve, press keys as shown.

Display answer: 1.78112

Answer: **$1.78**

Press Keys	Display Reads
5 · 0 6	5.06
×	5.06
4	4.
×	20.24
· 0 8 8	0.088
=	1.78112

Discovery

When you compute with paper and pencil, you total the number of decimal places in the problem to place the decimal point in the answer.

Pencil and Paper

$$\begin{array}{r} 6.84 \\ \times\ 3.7 \\ \hline 25.308 \end{array}$$

6.84 two places
× 3.7 + one place
25.308 three places
3 2 1

The calculator correctly places the decimal point for you.

A. Complete the following problems by correctly placing a decimal point in each answer. You will be able to catch keying errors on your calculator if you have a sense of where decimal points should be placed.

7.8	25.7	8.04	13.1	12.4
× 6	× .3	× .7	× 5.5	×.062
4 6 8	7 7 1	5 6 2 8	7 2 0 5	7 6 8 8

B. Calculate the exact answer. Then estimate an answer to check against possible keying errors.

	Exact	Estimate		Exact	Estimate		Exact	Estimate
1. a)	6.8	7	**b)**	8.12		**c)**	4.03	
	× 4.2	× 4		× .94			× 2.1	
		28						

2. a)	10.3		**b)**	12.9		**c)**	15.4	
	× 5.9			× 1.09			× 2.19	

C. Solve each of the following problems on your calculator. In rows 1 and 2, round each answer to the tenths place.

1. $7.5 \times 3.2 \times 6 =$ $9.6 \times 8.3 \times 5.7 =$

2. $21.4 \times 3.1 \times 5.2 =$ $31.5 \times 5.5 \times 3.2 =$

In row 3, round each answer to the nearest cent.

3. $\$2.75 \times 8.8 \times 4.6 =$ $\$15.45 \times 3.5 \times 5.25 =$

4. To the nearest cent, what will Beth pay for 16.4 gallons of gas bought at the Gas City pump price shown at right?

DIVIDING DECIMAL NUMBERS

As the following examples show, you can use your calculator to divide a decimal number by a whole number or to divide one decimal number by another.

- As in whole number division, your first step is to correctly identify the dividend and the divisor.

Example 1

7.894 ÷ 4

To solve, press the keys as shown.

Answer: **1.9735**

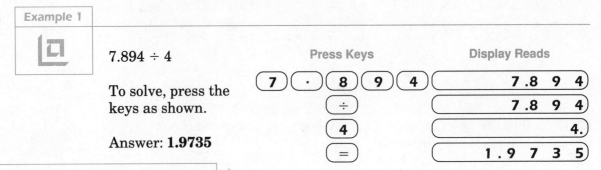

Press Keys	Display Reads
7 . 8 9 4	7.8 9 4
÷	7.8 9 4
4	4.
=	1.9 7 3 5

Discovery

A calculator carries out division until there is no remainder—or until the display is full. For this reason, the answer may contain more decimal places than the dividend (number being divided). See Examples 1 and 2.

Example 2

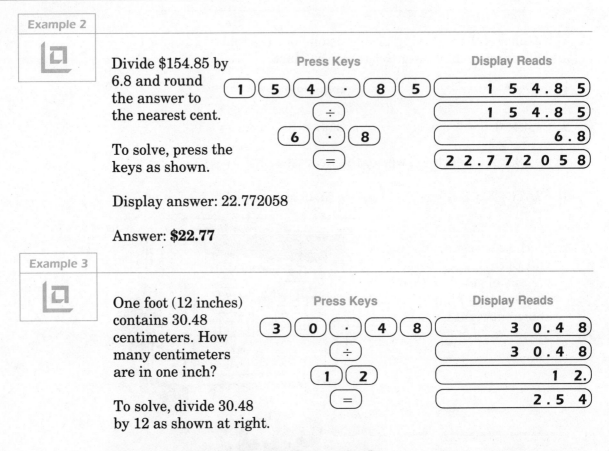

Divide $154.85 by 6.8 and round the answer to the nearest cent.

To solve, press the keys as shown.

Press Keys	Display Reads
1 5 4 . 8 5	1 5 4.8 5
÷	1 5 4.8 5
6 . 8	6.8
=	2 2.7 7 2 0 5 8

Display answer: 22.772058

Answer: **$22.77**

Example 3

One foot (12 inches) contains 30.48 centimeters. How many centimeters are in one inch?

To solve, divide 30.48 by 12 as shown at right.

Press Keys	Display Reads
3 0 . 4 8	3 0.4 8
÷	3 0.4 8
1 2	1 2.
=	2.5 4

Answer: **2.54 centimeters in one inch**

A. Identify the dividend (number being divided) and the divisor in the following problems. Circle the number you enter into your calculator first. **Do not solve.**

1. 6.54 ÷ 3.1 dividend _____

        divisor _____

2. 8 divided by 2.7 dividend _____

        divisor _____

B. Circle the answer choice that is the best estimate for each problem below. Estimating answers can help you to catch keying errors on the calculator.

1. 47.9 ÷ 6.1 **a)** 6
      b) 8
      c) 10

3. 104.8 ÷ 11.6 **a)** 5
       b) 10
       c) 15

2. 4.1$\overline{)33.7}$ **a)** 8
      b) 11
      c) 16

4. 8.01$\overline{)57.75}$ **a)** 3
       b) 5
       c) 7

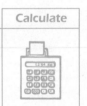

C. In row 1, round each answer to the 10ths place.

1. 363.2 ÷ 8.1 76.26 ÷ 3.14 12$\overline{)604.86}$ 13.8$\overline{)130.41}$

In row 2, round each answer to the 100ths place.

2. 78 ÷ 2.3 $24.71 ÷ 8 6$\overline{)\$142.88}$ 3.7$\overline{)8.93}$

3. Sherry bought a roast that was weighed on the scale at right. Fill in the $ PER LB. amount to show how much Sherry is paying per pound. Enter your answer to the nearest penny.

SCALE		
Total Price	$	21.60
5.87 LBS.	$	_._ _
Weight	$ PER LB.	

← Fill in this amount.

A. Circle the choice—a, b, or c—that best describes each correct answer. Hint: Estimate by substituting whole numbers for decimal numbers.

1. Working as a salesman, Geoff earned $64.24 in commissions Saturday during one 9-hour shift. On the average, how much did Geoff earn each hour in commissions?

   (Estimate: 63 ÷ 9)

   a) between $2 and $4
   b) between $4 and $6
   c) between $6 and $8

2. In the metric system, weight is measured in units called grams. If 28.4 grams is equal to 1 ounce, how many grams does an 11-ounce steak weigh?

   a) between 150 and 250
   b) between 250 and 350
   c) between 350 and 450

3. Joanne earns $6.86 an hour as a part-time hairstylist. At this rate, how much will Joanne earn in 7.25 hours?

   a) between $40 and $44
   b) between $48 and $52
   c) between $56 and $60

4. The distance between Mustafa's house and his office is 2.85 miles. He walks this distance twice each day, Monday through Friday. How many total miles does Mustafa walk each week between his house and work?

   a) between 12 and 18
   b) between 19 and 25
   c) between 26 and 32

5. Kerri paid $16.53 for a roast that was marked down from $24.95. The weight of the roast was 5.14 pounds. How much did Kerri pay per pound for this roast?

   a) between $3 and $4
   b) between $5 and $6
   c) between $7 and $8

B. First, use your calculator to compute an exact answer. Then estimate answers as a check against keying errors.

1. At Big Bear Foods, Vicki paid $1.19 for a sack of bananas. If the full sack weighed 2.9 pounds, how much did Vicki pay per pound?

   _____
   exact

   _____
   estimate

2. Yoshi's Import Foods received a box weighing 59.8 pounds that was filled with jars of pickled vegetables. If the box contains 22 jars, what is the weight of each jar to the nearest tenth pound? (Ignore the weight of the box itself.)

_____
exact

_____
estimate

3. As a decimal fraction, fifteen-sixteenths of an inch is written as .9375 inch. How wide would a group of eight paperback books be if each book is fifteen-sixteenths of an inch wide? (Write as a mixed decimal.)

_____
exact

_____
estimate

4. Water weighs approximately 8.3 pounds per gallon. Determine the weight of water in a hot water heater that contains 48 gallons when filled.

_____
exact

_____
estimate

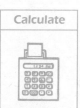

Calculate

C. Questions 1–4 refer to the following story. Use your calculator to compute answers to each question.

Anna is trying to decide which of two jobs to take. If she works for Data Systems, she'll be paid $5.44 an hour and work a standard 40-hour shift. However, a friend who works there has told Anna that Data almost always offers five hours of overtime work each week to each employee. Data pays an overtime pay rate of 1.5 times normal hourly wage.

Anna has also been offered a job at Brinson Electronics. At Brinson, Anna would be paid a weekly salary of $245.50 for 40 hours work. Brinson does not normally offer overtime work hours.

1. Not counting overtime, how much would Anna's weekly salary be at Data Systems?

2. Determine how much Anna would make for each hour of overtime at Data Systems.

3. Working five hours of overtime each week, how much total pay could Anna earn weekly at Data Systems?

4. Figure out how much Anna would make per hour if she decides to choose the job at Brinson.

FINDING AN AVERAGE

An average is a "typical" value. For example, suppose your electric bills during the summer months were as follows: June, $41.78; July, $46.12; and August, $38.34. Your average bill is easily computed:

- To compute the average of a group of numbers, add the numbers, and then divide the sum by the number of numbers in the group.

Step 1. Add the three bills.

$$\begin{array}{r} \$41.78 \\ 46.12 \\ + 38.34 \\ \hline \$126.24 \end{array}$$

Answer: **$42.08**

Step 2. Divide $126.24 by 3.

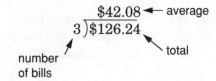

Discovery

An average is usually not equal in value to any of the numbers in the group you add. However, you'll discover that the average is often close to the middle value of the group.

Calculate

Use your calculator to answer each question below.

1. The three day-care centers near Mabel's home have monthly charges of $115.50, $118, and $112.25 for half-day child care. Determine the average cost of these centers.

2. Saturday night, Joel bowled four games and got these scores:
   first game: 168   second game: 179
   third game: 182   fourth game: 170
   To the nearest point, what was Joel's average score?

3. The price of a large pizza in Newport Beach varies quite a bit as prices at the right show. Determine the average price of a large pizza on this list.

Pizza Heaven	$14.75
Pizza Supreme	$12.80
Sparkey's Pizza	$16.00
Mama's Pizza	$13.90
Mario's Little Italy	$14.39

INTERPRETING A PAYCHECK STUB

An employer gives an employee a paycheck stub to tell the employee how much money is being withheld from his or her paycheck. The stub lists each **deduction** (withheld amount). Look at the paycheck stub below.

LAPINE MANUFACTURING

Employee: Jon Allen	Gross Pay	Federal Income Tax	State Income Tax	Social Security	Net Pay
Current Pay Period (two weeks)	$684.80	$79.24	$14.27	$51.72	$539.57
Year-to-Date	$8,217.60	$950.88	$171.24	$620.64	$6,474.84

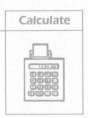

Write

A. Answer the questions below by filling in each blank with a number taken from the paycheck stub.

1. Gross pay is the total amount of money earned each pay period. **Net pay** is the actual amount of a paycheck.
net pay = gross pay − total deductions
What two ways can you use to determine Jon's total deductions for this pay period?
a) subtract _____ from _____, or
b) add _____, _____, and _____

2. Each **year-to-date** amount is the total sum of that amount starting with the mid-January pay period and including each pay period up through the present date.
Jon is paid the same amount for every pay period. To determine how many pay periods Jon has been paid this year, divide _____ by $684.80.

3. To determine how much total federal income tax will be withheld from Jon's check during an entire year, multiply _____ by 26 (the number of pay periods in one year).

Calculate

B. Use your calculator to help answer the following questions.

1. How much are Jon's total deductions for the pay period shown?

2. How many pay periods this year has Jon worked for Lapine?

3. If Jon works 78.5 hours each pay period, determine to the nearest penny Jon's
a) gross pay per hour   **b)** net pay per hour

4. About how much social security does Jon pay each year?

COMPARING COSTS OF CHILD CARE

Child care is an expense for many families. One important step in choosing a child care center is to compare the costs of different centers. The exercise on this page deals with this type of comparison.

Sheri Robertson is a single parent who needs child care for her daughter Ashley for three months in the summer— June, July, and August. She wants Ashley to eat lunch each day at the center.

As shown below, Sheri made a list of the costs of sending Ashley to each of the two centers in her community. Ashley would be using transportation at either center.

	Super Kids Care	**Huggy Bear Center**
Registration Fee (one-time fee, paid the first month)	$18.00	$35.00
Childcare	$187.95/month	$11.85/day*
Transportation (only charged for days of attendance)	$2.75/day*	$1.50/day*

*Figure that every month has 20 working days.

Calculate

Use your calculator to help determine each of the costs indicated below.

	At Super Kids	At Huggy Bear

1. June's total costs: _____ _____

2. Total costs for July and August together: _____ _____

3. Total costs for three-month summer attendance: _____ _____

4. What is the difference in total costs between the two choices that Sheri has listed? _____

COMPARING ANNUAL CAR COSTS

For his new business, Sherm Harland has decided to buy one of two used pickup trucks. His decision will be based on a comparison of first–year costs of each truck.

Calculate

Using your calculator, complete the lists of first-year costs of each truck described below. Fill in the correct amount on each blank line.

Immediate Costs	CHEVROLET	FORD
Selling price	$1,645.00	$1,975.00
License & regis.	32.50	32.50
Tune–Up	49.95	64.95
New tires	329.88	none
Radiator repair	78.99	none
Brake repair	none	138.49
New muffler	29.99	35.99
1. Insurance premium (every three months)	$93.19 _____ (yearly)	$102.58 _____ (yearly)
2. **Total Immediate Costs:**	_____	_____

Operating Expenses		
Gas Expense:		
Estimated yearly mileage	12,000	12,000
Miles per gallon	17	14
3. Number of gallons needed (to nearest gallon)	_____	_____
Cost per gallon	$1.17	$1.17
4. Total cost of gas (to nearest cent)	_____	_____
Oil Expense:		
5. Three oil changes at $19.95 each	_____	_____
6. **Total Operating Expenses:**	_____	_____
7. **Total First–Year Costs:** (Add line 2 and line 6.)	_____	_____

A fraction, like a decimal, stands for part of a whole. A fraction is written as one number over another.

$\frac{3 \leftarrow \text{numerator}}{4 \leftarrow \text{denominator}}$

The numerator tells how many parts you have. The denominator tells how many parts one whole is divided into.

Types of Common Fractions

Common fractions are written in one of three ways:

- As a **proper fraction** in which the top number is always smaller than the bottom number.

  Example 1: $\frac{2}{3}$

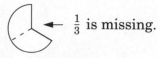

$\frac{1}{3}$ is missing.

$\frac{2}{3}$ of a pie is shown.

- As an **improper fraction** in which the top number is the same as or larger than the bottom number.

  Example 2: $\frac{5}{3}$

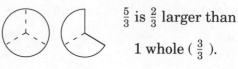

$\frac{5}{3}$ is $\frac{2}{3}$ larger than 1 whole ($\frac{3}{3}$).

$\frac{5}{3}$ pies are shown.

- As part of a **mixed number**, which is a whole number together with a proper fraction.

  Example 3: $1\frac{3}{4}$

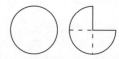

$1\frac{3}{4}$ pies are shown.

Changing Common Fractions to Decimal Fractions

You can use your calculator to change fractions to decimals:

- To change a common fraction to a decimal fraction, divide the denominator into the numerator.

Example 1

Change $\frac{9}{16}$ to a decimal fraction.

Divide 9 by 16 by pressing the keys shown.

Answer: $\frac{9}{16}$ = **0.5625**

Press Keys	Display Reads
9	9.
÷	9.
1 6	1 6.
=	0.5625

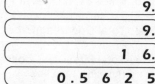

- To compare a common fraction with a decimal fraction, change the
  common fraction to a decimal fraction.

Example 2

Which is larger, $\frac{11}{16}$ or 0.65?

Step 1: Write $\frac{11}{16}$ as a decimal fraction.

As shown at right, $\frac{11}{16} = 0.6875$.

Step 2: To compare 0.6875 with 0.65,
give each the same number of
decimal places. Do this by adding two 0's to 0.65:
$0.65 = 0.6500$

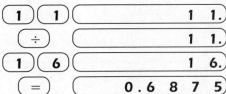

Press Keys	Display Reads
1 1	1 1.
÷	1 1.
1 6	1 6.
=	0 . 6 8 7 5

Answer: **0.6875 ($\frac{11}{16}$) is larger** than 0.65 because 6875 is larger than 6500.

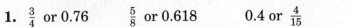

Calculate

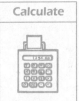

A. Using your calculator to change each common fraction to a decimal
fraction, circle the larger number in each pair below.

1. $\frac{3}{4}$ or 0.76 $\frac{5}{8}$ or 0.618   0.4 or $\frac{4}{15}$ 0.865 or $\frac{5}{7}$

For problems in row 2, change both fractions to decimals and then
compare. Circle the larger fraction.

2. $\frac{2}{3}$ or $\frac{3}{5}$ $\frac{9}{17}$ or $\frac{6}{13}$ $\frac{21}{32}$ or $\frac{2}{3}$ $\frac{8}{10}$ or $\frac{51}{64}$

B. Solve each word problem below.

1. Which of the following is the larger amount: $0.35 or $\frac{3}{8}$ of a dollar?

2. Cal needs to drill a hole that will
   allow a 0.2 inch diameter wire to
   pass through. He wants the wire
   to fit the hole as tightly as possible.
   Which of the three drill bits will
   give the wire the tightest fit?

Bit #	Diameter
#1	$\frac{3}{16}$ inch
#2	$\frac{7}{32}$ inch
#3	$\frac{13}{64}$ inch

3. Will a bridge that has a load limit of $5\frac{2}{3}$ tons safely support a
   loaded truck that weighs 5.754 tons?

CALCULATIONS WITH FRACTIONS

Fractions and mixed numbers can be added, subtracted, multiplied, and divided. Below are examples of paper-and-pencil solutions.

Addition	Subtraction	Multiplication	Division
$\frac{2}{3} = \frac{10}{15}$	$1\frac{1}{2} = \frac{3}{2} = \frac{9}{6}$	$2\frac{3}{4} \times \frac{7}{8}$	$\frac{2}{5} \div 2\frac{1}{4}$
$+ \frac{3}{5} = \frac{9}{15}$	$- \frac{5}{6} = \frac{5}{6}$	$= \frac{11}{4} \times \frac{7}{8}$	$= \frac{2}{5} \div \frac{9}{4}$
$\frac{19}{15} = 1\frac{4}{15}$	$\frac{4}{6} = \frac{2}{3}$	$= \frac{77}{32}$	$= \frac{2}{5} \times \frac{4}{9}$
		$= 2\frac{13}{32}$	$= \frac{8}{45}$

CALCULATORS AND COMMON FRACTIONS

Unfortunately, most calculators are not designed to do calculations like those above. On calculators that are, the keying is often more difficult than pencil and paper solutions!

Even though your calculator may not solve fraction problems directly, you can still use it to solve fraction problems indirectly in two situations:

- when a decimal answer is required
- when you are given answer choices

Example 1

$2 \times 3\frac{5}{12}$

a) $6\frac{1}{2}$ **b)** $6\frac{2}{3}$ **c)** $6\frac{5}{6}$

Step 1. Change $3\frac{5}{12}$ to a mixed decimal. Start with changing the fraction to a decimal.
$\frac{5}{12} = 5 \div 12 \approx .42$

$\boxed{0.4166666}$ or $\boxed{0.42}$
displayed   rounded

$3\frac{5}{12} \approx \boxed{3.42}$

Step 2. Multiply by 2.
$3.42 \times 2 = 6.84$

$\boxed{6.84}$
estimated answer

Step 3. Convert the other mixed fractions to decimals and compare.

a) $6\frac{1}{2} = \boxed{6.5} = 6.5$
b) $6\frac{2}{3} = \boxed{6.6666666} \approx 6.67$
c) $6\frac{5}{6} = \boxed{6.8333333} \approx 6.83$

Answer: $6.84 \approx 6.83$, so **c) $6\frac{5}{6}$ is correct.**

Example 2

Matt bought $2\frac{1}{2}$ lbs. of apples and $6\frac{2}{3}$ pounds of cherries. How much fruit did he buy?

a) $9\frac{1}{6}$ lbs.   **b)** $9\frac{1}{2}$ lbs.   **c)** $9\frac{1}{3}$ lbs.

Step 1. Change the mixed fractions to decimals.

$2\frac{1}{2} = \boxed{2.5} = 2.5$

$6\frac{2}{3} = \boxed{6.6666666} \approx 6.67$

Step 2. Add the mixed decimals.

$2.5 + 6.67 = 9.17$

$\boxed{9.17}$

estimated answer

Step 3. Convert the other mixed fractions and compare.

a) $9\frac{1}{6} = \boxed{9.1666666} \approx 9.17$

b) $9\frac{1}{2} = \boxed{9.5} = 9.5$

c) $9\frac{1}{3} = \boxed{9.3333333} \approx 9.3$

Answer: **a) 9.17 lbs.** ($9\frac{1}{6}$ lbs.)

Use your calculator to solve each problem below.

In problems 1–4, circle your answer from the choices given.

1. $\begin{array}{r} 4\frac{3}{8} \\ + \\ 3\frac{5}{6} \\ \hline \end{array}$

   a) $7\frac{43}{48}$

   b) $7\frac{11}{12}$

   c) $8\frac{5}{24}$

3. $\begin{array}{r} 9\frac{6}{7} \\ - \\ 3\frac{4}{5} \\ \hline \end{array}$

   a) $6\frac{2}{35}$

   b) $6\frac{6}{35}$

   c) $6\frac{9}{35}$

2. $4 \times 3\frac{2}{3} =$

   a) $14\frac{1}{3}$

   b) $14\frac{2}{3}$

   c) $14\frac{5}{6}$

4. $6\frac{4}{5} \div 3 =$

   a) $2\frac{1}{6}$

   b) $2\frac{4}{15}$

   c) $2\frac{5}{12}$

5. Linda paid $9.57 for $12\frac{3}{4}$ pounds of peaches. To the nearest penny, how much is Linda paying per pound?

CALCULATOR TIC-TAC-TOE

Choose another student or friend to play Calculator Tic-tac-toe with you. Use pencils and mark the board lightly so that marks can be erased. You can play this game numerous times.

109.4	18	47.43
5.1	70.1	57.7
89.9	143.5	10

a) 35.8 + 97.3

b) 41.4 + 28.7

c) 88.9 − 31.2

d) 64.9 − 49.8

e) 97.8 + 31.4 + 28.2

f) 57.8 + 46.3 + 39.4

g) 100 − 57.3 − 26.8

h) 200 − 62.7 − 27.9

i) 11.9 × 21.6

j) 5.8 × 5 × 3.1

k) 9.3 × 5.1

l) 46.92 ÷ 9.2

m) 73.71 ÷ 9.1

n) 7.2 × 2.5

o) $7 \times 4\frac{3}{7}$

p) 3.5 ÷ .35

Rules: **1)** The goal of each player is to place his or her initials on a row of three squares. The row can be across, up and down, or on a diagonal.

2) Player A chooses a letter from *a* to *p* and then does the calculation. If the calculated answer is one of the numbers in a square, Player A places his or her initials on that square. It then becomes Player B's turn.

If Player A chooses a problem whose answer is not in a square, Player A loses that turn and it becomes Player B's turn.

3) Players alternate turns until one player completes a row of three squares. That player is then the winner.

Hint: A player is allowed to make mental estimates of answers before doing a calculation. Using estimates, a player can first pick a square and then try to find a problem whose answer will match that square.

PART 4

Percents

Percents are a part of daily life. We use them to pay taxes and to calculate interest payments. Two items can make percents easier to use—your calculator and a memory device called the **percent circle.**

In the next several pages, you will learn to use both of these tools to master percents.

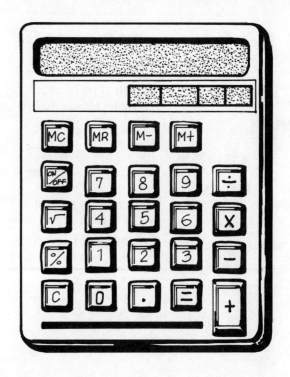

The three main types of percent problems are listed below. They are based on this statement: 25% of $300 is $75.

- Finding **part** of a whole.
  What is 25% of $300? **$75**

- Finding what **percent** a part is of a whole.
  What percent of $300 is $75? **25%**

- Finding a **whole** when a part of it is given.
  Example: If 25% of the price is $75, what is the total price? **$300**

In a percent problem, you are given two of these factors (part, percent, or whole), and you must find the third.

The Percent Circle

On the pages ahead, we'll show you how a calculator can simplify solving each type of percent problem. On those pages we'll refer to a memory device shown below called the **percent circle.**

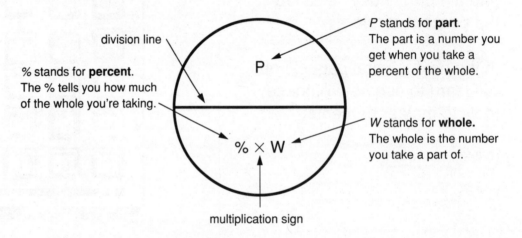

division line

% stands for **percent**.
The % tells you how much of the whole you're taking.

P stands for **part**.
The part is a number you get when you take a percent of the whole.

W stands for **whole.**
The whole is the number you take a part of.

multiplication sign

The following three examples show how the percent circle can help you remember how to find the part, the percent, or the whole.

| Example 1 |

Finding **part** of the whole

If 25% of your $300 check is withheld for taxes, how much is withheld?

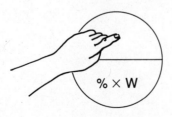

Cover the P (part), the number you are trying to find. The uncovered symbols tell you this is a **multiplication problem:**
$P = \% \times W$
$P = 25\% \times \$300$

Example 2

Finding the **percent**

In just over three months, Amy lost 40 pounds. If she originally weighed 200 pounds, what percent of her weight did she lose?

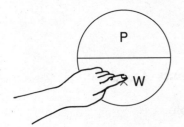

Cover the % (percent), the number you are trying to find. The uncovered symbols tell you this is a **division problem:**

$\% = P \div W$

$\% = 40 \div 200$

Example 3

Finding the **whole**

When he bought a used piano, Willis paid $245 as a down payment. If this payment is 15% of the price of the piano, what was the full price of the piano?

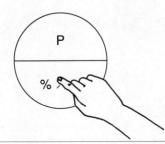

Cover the W (whole), the number you are trying to find. The uncovered symbols tell you this is a **division problem:**

$W = P \div \%$

$W = \$245 \div 15\%$

In each problem below, use the percent circle to determine what it is you're asked to find and circle your answer choice: **part, percent,** or **whole.** Then, place a check to indicate whether the problem is solved by multiplication or division.

1. Jimi had to pay a $.42 sales tax when he bought lunch for $7.00. What tax rate did Jimi pay?

    a) part
    b) percent
    c) whole

_____ multiplication   _____ division

2. Each month, Arnie saves 9% of his net pay. If his monthly net pay is $845, how much is Arnie able to save each month?

    a) part
    b) percent
    c) whole

_____ multiplication   _____ division

3. To pass her math test, Francine needs to answer 36 questions correctly. If 36 questions is 60% of the test, how many questions are on the test?

    a) part
    b) percent
    c) whole

_____ multiplication   _____ division

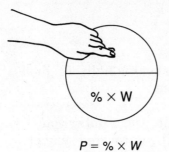

$$P = \% \times W$$

> **How to Do It**
>
> To find part of a whole, multiply the whole by the percent.

Here are the steps for using a calculator to find part of a whole:

Step 1. Enter the number representing the whole.

Step 2. Press the $\times$ key.

Step 3. Enter the number of the percent.

Step 4. Press the % key. **On most calculators, pressing** % **completes the calculation. On some calculators, you need to press** % **and** $=$.

Work through the following examples to see if the % key or the $=$ finishes your calculation.

Example 1

Find 25% of 70.

On Calculator

Step 1. Identify % and W.
% = 25% W = 70
P = unknown part

Step 2. Multiply 70 × 25% on your calculator.

Press Keys	Display Reads
7 0	7 0.
×	7 0.
2 5	2 5.
% *	1 7 . 5

Answer: **17.5**

Compare with Pencil and Paper Solution

Step 1. Identify % and W.
% = 25% W = 70
P = unknown part

Step 2. Change 25% to a decimal by moving the decimal point two places to the left.
25% = .25

Step 3. Multiply 70 by .25.

$$
\begin{array}{r}
7\,0 \\
\times\ .2\,5 \\
\hline
3\,5\,0 \\
1\,4\,0 \\
\hline
1\,7.5\,0 = \textbf{17.5}
\end{array}
$$

Discovery

Try pressing keys in this order:

2 5 %
× 7 0 =

What happens? Most calculators display "0"! Remember: To do percent problems correctly, enter whole numbers first.

---

* On some calculators, you may need to press $=$ to complete the calculation.

Example 2

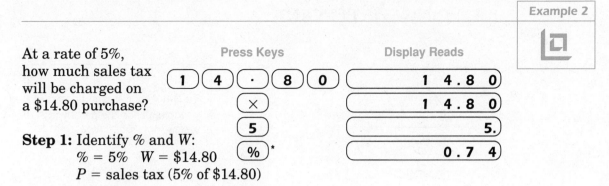

At a rate of 5%, how much sales tax will be charged on a $14.80 purchase?

Press Keys	Display Reads
1 4 · 8 0	1 4 . 8 0
×	1 4 . 8 0
5	5.
% *	0 . 7 4

Step 1: Identify % and W:
  % = 5%   W = $14.80
  P = sales tax (5% of $14.80)

Step 2: To solve on your calculator, multiply $14.80 by 5% as shown at right.

Answer: **$.74**

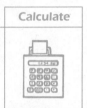

Calculate

Use your calculator to find each number indicated below. The correct keying order is shown for the first problem in each row.

Percents Between 1% and 100%

1. 20% of 90   35% of 240   8% of $25.50   75% of 88
   9 0 × 2 0 % *

2. 92% of 400   12% of $345   50% of 548   4% of $35.50
   4 0 0 × 9 2 % *

Decimal Percents

3. .5% of $4   .7% of 85   5.5% of $30   3.4% of 62
   4 × · 5 % *

Percents Larger Than 100%

4. 250% of 18   300% of $58   150% of 90   200% of $56
   1 8 × 2 5 0 % *

5. Each week, Kyle saves 15% of his $243.60 paycheck. What amount is Kyle able to save each week?

6. When his $460 property tax bill goes up by 2.5%, how much additional property tax will Kiwon have to pay?

7. If she makes a commission of 3.5% on each sale, how much commission will Sarah earn for selling a $598 couch?

* On some calculators, you may need to press (=) to complete the calculation.

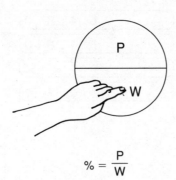

$$\% = \frac{P}{W}$$

> **How to Do It**
>
> To find what percent a part is of a whole, divide the part by the whole.

Here are the steps for using a calculator to find the percent:

Step 1. Enter the number representing the part.

Step 2. Press the (÷) key.

Step 3. Enter the whole.

Step 4. Press the (%) key. **On most calculators, pressing (%) completes the calculation. On some calculators, you need to press (%) and (=) to finish the calculation.**

As the final key pressed, the (%) key tells the calculator to do the division and to express the answer as a percent.

Example 1

12 is what percent of 60?

On Calculator	**Compare with Pencil and Paper Solution**
Step 1. Identify P and W. $P = 12$ $W = 60$ $\%$ = unknown percent	**Step 1.** Identify P and W. $P = 12$ $W = 60$ $\%$ = unknown percent
Step 2. Divide 12 by 60, pressing (%) to tell the calculator to write the answer as a percent.	**Step 2.** Divide 12 by 60. $$60 \overline{)12.0}^{\,.2}$$

Discovery

Although your calculator has a (%) key, no % symbol appears on the display.

Press Keys	Display Reads
(1)(2)	1 2.
(÷)	1 2.
(6)(0)	6 0.
(%)*	2 0.

Step 3. Change .2 to a percent by moving the decimal point two places to the right and adding a percent sign.

$$.2 = .20\%$$

Answer: **20%**

Answer: **20%**

The same keying is used to change a common fraction to an equivalent percent. When you change a fraction to a percent, you are really asking, "What percent of the denominator (bottom number) is the numerator (top number)?"

Example 2

Change $\frac{3}{4}$ to an equivalent percent.

Step 1: Identify P and W:
    $P = 3$ $W = 4$
    $\% =$ unknown percent

Step 2: To solve on your calculator, divide 3 by 4 and press $\boxed{\%}$* as shown at right

Press Keys	Display Reads
3	3.
÷	3.
4	4.
%	7 5.

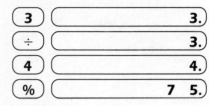

Answer: **75%**

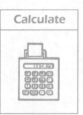

Use your calculator to find each percent. The correct keying order is shown for selected problems.

1. 8 is what percent of 40?
    ⑧⊘④⓪%*

2. 20 is what percent of 25?

3. What percent of 50 is 19?
    ①⑨⊘⑤⓪%*

4. What percent of 95 is 38?

5. 45 is what percent of 75?

6. To the nearest percent, 9 is what percent of 28?

7. What percent of 64 is 32?

8. To the nearest tenth of a percent, what percent of 145 is 75?

Change each fraction below to an equivalent percent.

9. $\frac{1}{4} =$ $\frac{3}{5} =$ $\frac{9}{20} =$ $\frac{7}{10} =$ $\frac{14}{35} =$
    ①⊘④%*

To the nearest tenth of a percent, change each fraction below to an equivalent percent.

10. $\frac{3}{8} =$ $\frac{5}{16} =$ $\frac{1}{3} =$ $\frac{3}{32} =$ $\frac{2}{3} =$

11. Out of each $300 paycheck, José's employer withholds $42 for federal income tax. What percent of José's check is withheld for this tax?

12. After riding 10 miles, Louise had completed $\frac{2}{5}$ of the bicycle race. At this point, what percent of the race had Louise completed?

* On some calculators, you may need to press $\boxed{=}$ to complete the calculation.

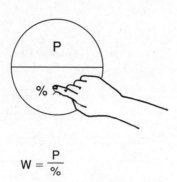

$$W = \frac{P}{\%}$$

> **How to Do It**
>
> To find a whole when part of it is given, divide the part by the percent.

When using a calculator to find the whole, follow these steps:

Step 1. Enter the number representing the part.

Step 2. Press the $\div$ key.

Step 3. Enter the number of the percent.

Step 4. Press the $\%$ key. **On most calculators, pressing $\%$ completes the calculation. On some calculators, you need to press $=$ to complete the calculation.**

As Example 1 below shows, when the percent is less than 100%, your answer (the whole) will be larger than the part you start with.

Example 1

16 is 20% of what number? (Or, asked another way, 20% of what number is 16?)

On Calculator	Compare with Pencil and Paper Solution
Step 1. Identify P and %. $P = 16$ % = 20% W = unknown whole	**Step 1.** Identify P and %. $P = 16$ % = 20% W = unknown whole
Step 2. Divide 16 by 20% on your calculator.	**Step 2.** Change 20% to a decimal by moving the decimal point two places to the left.

Discovery

You may notice that the order of keying used to find the whole *is the same as that used to find the* percent *(discussed on page 82). Be aware of this—but not confused by it! Think of it as simplifying your work!*

Press Keys	Display Reads
1 6	1 6.
÷	1 6.
2 0	2 0.
%*	8 0.

$20\% = .20$

Step 3. Divide 16 by .20.

$$.20\overline{)16.00} \quad \begin{array}{c} 80. \end{array}$$

Answer: **80**

Answer: **80**

Example 2

The sale price of a TV is $289. If $289 is 80% of the original price, what did the TV cost before the sale?

Step 1: Identify P and %.
$P = \$289$ % = 80%
W = original price

Step 2: To solve on your calculator, divide 289 by 80% as shown at right.

Press Keys	Display Reads
2 8 9	2 8 9.
÷	2 8 9.
8 0	8 0.
% *	3 6 1 . 2 5

Answer: **$361.25**

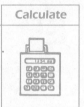
Calculate

Using your calculator, solve each problem below. The correct keying order is shown for problems 2 and 4.

1. 25% of what number is 67?

2. 5.7% of what number is 57?
5 7 ÷ 5 · 7 % *

3. $14 is 50% of what amount?

4. 52.5 is 35% of what number?
5 2 · 5 ÷ 3 5 % *

5. 12% of what number is 30?

6. 7.5% of what amount is $150?

7. $32 is 80% of what amount?

8. $90 is 3.6% of what amount?

9. During May, Opal lost six pounds, which is 30% of the weight she hopes to lose on her diet. How many pounds does Opal hope to lose in all?

10. For the month of January, Guy paid $9.90 in interest charges on his Visa card. Guy pays 1.5% interest charges each month on any unpaid balance. Given these figures, determine the amount of Guy's unpaid balance for the month of January.

11. Darla bought a toaster at the sale shown at right. Before the sale, what was the price of this toaster?

TOASTER SALE

You pay only
70%
of original price

Sale Price
$12.60

* On some calculators, you may need to press (=) to complete the calculation.

Many percent problems involve increasing or decreasing a whole by a part. For example, suppose you want to find the purchase price of a sweater in a state where there is a 5% sales tax. Without a calculator, this takes two steps:

- First, you must find the amount of the sales tax (the part).

- Second, you must add the sales tax to the selling price (the whole).

As the example below shows, your calculator combines these two steps into a single step. This single step is much easier and faster.

Example 1

In a state with a 5% sales tax, what is the purchase price of a sweater selling for $29.60?

On Calculator

Step 1. Identify % and W.
% = 5%   W = $29.60

Step 2. On your calculator, you add $29.60 and 5% of $29.60. The complete calculation is done by pressing the keys shown below!

Press Keys	Display Reads
2 9 · 6 0	2 9 . 6 0
+	2 9 . 6 0
5	5.
% *	3 1 . 0 8

Answer: **$31.08**

Compare with Pencil and Paper Solution

Step 1. Identify % and W.
% = 5%
W = $29.60

Step 2. Change 5% to a decimal.
5% = .05

Step 3. To find the sales tax, multiply $29.60 by .05.

$$\begin{array}{r} \$29.60 \\ \times\ .05 \\ \hline 1.48\ 00 = \$1.48 \end{array}$$

Step 4. To find the purchase price, add the sales tax ($1.48) to the selling price ($29.60).

$$\begin{array}{r} \$29.60 \\ +\ 1.48 \\ \hline \$31.08 \end{array}$$

Answer: **$31.08**

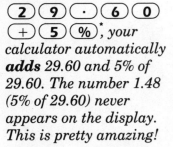

Discovery

When you press
2 9 · 6 0
+ 5 % *, your calculator automatically **adds** 29.60 and 5% of 29.60. The number 1.48 (5% of 29.60) never appears on the display. This is pretty amazing!*

*To **subtract** 5%, press*
2 9 · 6 0
− 5 % *. Your calculator will automatically subtract 1.48 (5% of 29.60) from 29.60.*

* On some calculators, you may need to press (=) to complete the calculation.

Below are several types of problems in which you increase or decrease the whole with your calculator:

- To solve an **increase** problem, add the percent.
- To solve a **decrease** problem, subtract the percent.

> RATE INCREASE: New amount = original amount + amount of increase

1. Before the price increase, Benji's Market sold oat bran for 90¢ per pound. After he raised the price by 10%, what was Benji's per pound price for oat bran?

2. In 1980 the population of North Oswego was 48,600. By 1990 the population had risen 24%. In 1990, what was the population of North Oswego?

> RATE DECREASE: New amount = original amount − amount of decrease

3. Before Van agreed to an 8.5% pay cut, her yearly income was $13,432. Determine the yearly income she'll receive after the pay cut.

4. Due to an unusually warm winter, the Thurmans' January heating bill was 30% lower this year than last year. If last year's January bill was $184.60, how much did they pay this January?

> MARKUP: Selling price = store's cost + markup

5. Lucky Saver Stores places a 15% markup on every item they sell. Knowing this, determine the price Lucky Saver will charge for a pair of work boots that cost Lucky Saver $24.60.

6. At Fran's Clothes Closet, Fran pays $56.00 for the Paris Nights evening gowns that she sells. If Fran adds a 30% markup to her cost, what price does she ask for these gowns?

> DISCOUNT: Sale price = original price − amount of discount

7. At a "Saturday Only Sale," Special Electronics is offering a discount of 25% on all store merchandise. At this sale, what will be the price of a car stereo that normally sells for $149.80?

8. The Car Place offers a 10% discount on a case (12 quarts) of car oil. If the regular price is $1.18 per quart, or $14.16 per case, what is the discount price on a full case? Express your answer to the nearest penny.

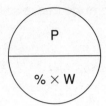

Refer to this percent circle as you solve the problems below. In your future work with percents, you may want to draw yourself a percent circle.

Write:

A. Problems 1–4 are designed to improve your estimation skills; use only common sense to answer these questions. For each problem below, circle the choice—a, b, or c—that best describes the correct answer.

1. Forty-two families send children to Little Cubs Preschool. If 100% of these families attended the school Christmas party, how many families attended in all?

   a) fewer than 42
   b) exactly 42
   c) more than 42

2. Of the 24 children in Mrs. Grey's fourth grade class, 18 are able to swim. What percent of Mrs. Grey's students can swim?

   a) less than 100%
   b) exactly 100%
   c) more than 100%

3. In June, Shelley is getting a 7% raise. What will Shelley's monthly salary be in June if now, in April, she is making $860 per month?

   a) less than $860
   b) exactly $860
   c) more than $860

4. Fourteen of the 34 workers at Emerald Tree Farm have a native language other than English. What percent of the work force do these 14 workers represent?

   a) less than 100%
   b) exactly 100%
   c) more than 100%

Calculate

B. Use your calculator to solve each problem below. As a first step, decide if you are looking for the part, the percent, the whole, or an increase or decrease. Then use the percent circle above to decide to multiply or divide.

1. When he bought his new washing machine, Freddie paid a 15% down payment cost of $48. What price did Freddie agree to pay for this appliance?

2. During the primary election, 45% of the 34,600 registered voters in Harper County voted. How many people voted in this election?

3. After the new drunk driver laws went into effect this year, traffic accidents in Lake County decreased by 20% each month. How many traffic accidents occurred in Lake County this July if 75 accidents occurred last July?

4. After paying his bills each month, Bernie has $426 left out of a monthly paycheck of $1,154. To the nearest percent, what percent of Bernie's paycheck is not eaten up by bills?

5. At a Memorial Day sale, Glenda saw a coat marked with two tags. One read, "Price $84.00." The other read, "Take an additional 20% off the marked price." If she buys the coat, what can Glenda expect to pay?

6. When she bought a blouse for $28.80, Leona was told that she was paying only 80% of the original price. If this is true, what was the price of the blouse before it was marked down?

7. In an attempt to increase business, Tino has lowered the price of pizzas as shown at right. What percent decrease does the price change in the medium size pizzas represent? (Hint: Percent decrease = amount of decrease divided by original amount.)

Tino's Pizza Price Reduction!		
	Old Price	New Price
Large	$14.75	$13.25
Medium	$12.50	$11.25
Small	$ 9.85	$ 8.45

Questions 8–9 refer to the graph below.

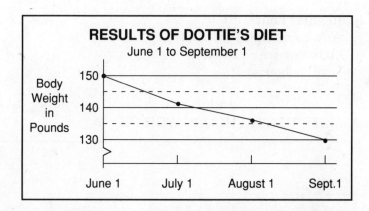

RESULTS OF DOTTIE'S DIET
June 1 to September 1

8. To the nearest percent, what percent of her June 1st body weight did Dottie lose between June 1st and September 1st?

9. On January 1st, before she started her diet, Dottie's weight was actually 4% less than her June 1st weight. Determine Dottie's weight on January 1st.

COMPLETING PAYROLL FORMS

Calculators are being used widely in many workplaces, especially for repetitive tasks. A repetitive calculator task is one in which you make similar calculations over and over again.

A calculator really simplifies the work of filling out a company's payroll forms. Each employee's hours must be added, and both total pay (**gross pay**) and **net pay** must be calculated.

In exercises A and B below, you'll use your calculator to help you fill out the weekly payroll forms of Harding Tool Company. At Harding, a regular work week is 40 hours. Any hours beyond 40 are paid at an overtime rate of 1.5 times the regular hourly rate (commonly called "time and a half").

For fun, time yourself on these two exercises. When you finish, estimate how long it would take you to do a 50-person payroll!

Calculate

A. In this first exercise, you are to fill in the Determining Hours Worked chart. Write your answers on the blank lines provided. As a guide, Laurie Allen's row has been filled in for you. The calculations used to fill in this row are as follows:

Example: Hours for Laurie Allen

Step 1. Total hours: <u>45</u>
Add: 8.0 + 8.0 + 9.0 + 9.5 + 7.5 + 3.0

Step 3. Overtime Hours: <u>5</u>
Subtract: 45 − 40

Step 2. Regular hours: <u>40</u>
Any hours up to the first 40 hours are counted as regular hours.

Discovery

As you work these exercises, keep your eye on the display to avoid simple keying errors. Be sure you enter the numbers you intend to.

DETERMINING HOURS WORKED

Name	M	T	W	T	F	S	S	① Total Hours	② Regular Hours	③ Overtime Hours
Allen	8.0	8.0	9.0	9.5	7.5	3.0		_45_	_40_	_5_
Cook	8.0	9.5	6.5	9.0	8.5	2.5	2.5	___	_40_	___
Dart	7.5	9.0	5.5	7.5	6.5			___	_36_	___
Franks		8.5	7.5	8.5	9.0	8.5	3.5	___	_40_	___
Norris	9.0	8.5	8.0	5.5	7.5	8.5		___	_40_	___

B. In this exercise, you are to fill in the Determining Net Pay chart. The first step is to compute the net pay for each employee. Again, Laurie Allen's row has been filled in for you as an example. The calculations used to fill in this row are as follows.

Example: Net pay for Laurie Allen

Step 1. Regular hours: <u>40</u>
Information taken from the Hours Worked Chart, page 90

Step 2. Regular pay rate: <u>$5.32</u>
Information provided on the Net Pay Chart below

Step 3. Total regular pay: <u>$212.80</u>
Multiply: $5.32 × 40 (hours)

Step 4. Overtime hours: <u>5</u>
Information taken from the Hours Worked Chart, page 90

Step 5. Overtime pay rate: <u>$7.98</u>
Multiply: $5.32 × 1.5 (Time & 1/2)

Step 6. Total overtime pay: $39.90
Multiply $7.98 × 5 (overtime hours)

Step 7. Total pay: <u>$252.70</u>
Add $212.80 + $39.90

Step 8. Total % withholding: <u>14%</u>
Information provided on the Net Pay Chart below

Step 9. Net Pay: <u>$217.32</u>
Subtract 14% of $252.70 from $252.70 (Hint: ②⑤②· ⑦⓪⊖①④%; review page 86) (Answer: **$217.322 rounds to $217.32.**)

When you are done finding each employee's net pay, fill in the bottom of the chart.

DETERMINING NET PAY

Name	① Regular Hours	② Regular Pay Rate	③ Total Regular Pay	④ Overtime Hours	⑤ Overtime Pay Rate	⑥ Total Overtime Pay	⑦ Total Pay	⑧ Total % Withholding	⑨ Net Pay
Allen	40	$5.32	$212.80	5	$7.98	$39.90	$252.70	14%	$217.32
Cook	___	$5.32	___	___	___	___	___	14%	___
Dart	___	$6.28	___	___	___	___	___	16%	___
Franks	___	$6.48	___	___	___	___	___	16%	___
Norris	___	$7.94	___	___	___	___	___	18%	___

Total Regular Hours For All Workers _____
   (ADD COLUMN 1)
Total Overtime Hours For All Workers _____
   (ADD COLUMN 4)
Total Regular Pay For All Workers _____
   (ADD COLUMN 3)

Total Net Pay For All Workers _____
   (ADD COLUMN 9)
Total Overtime Pay For All Workers _____
   (ADD COLUMN 6)

COMPUTING SIMPLE INTEREST**

Interest is money that is earned (or paid) for the use of money.

- If you deposit money in a savings account, interest is money that the bank pays you for using your money.

- If you borrow money or charge purchases on a credit card, interest is money that you pay the lender or charge-card company.

Simple interest is interest on a **principal** (the original amount borrowed or deposited). To compute simple interest, we use the **simple interest formula.** In words: Interest equals **P**rincipal times **R**ate times **T**ime. In symbols, the formula is: $I = PRT$.

Interest (I)	=	Principal (P)	×	Rate (R)	×	Time (T)
Expressed in dollars		Expressed in dollars		Expressed as a percent		Expressed in years

Example

Tani deposited $600 in a savings account that pays 5.5% simple interest. How much interest will Tani's account earn in 3 years?

Step 1. Identify P, R, and T.
$P = \$600$ $R = 5.5\%$
$T = 3$

Step 2. To find I, use $I = PRT$.
Interest =
$600 \times 5.5\% \times 3$

When you press (%), the display reads 33, the interest earned in only one year.

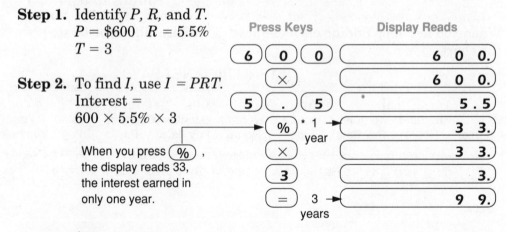

Answer: **$99**

Note: Don't confuse the use of the letter P in the simple interest formula with its use in the percent circle. In I = PRT, P stands for *principal*. In the percent circle, P stands for *part*.

* On some calculators, you may need to press (=) to complete the calculation.

**In actual practice, banks use a more complicated interest formula called the **compound interest formula. Compound interest will be discussed on page 122.

Although interest is earned (or paid) at a yearly rate, some deposits and loans are for part of a year. When using the simple interest formula, you change the part of a year to a decimal fraction. Remember, one month = $\frac{1}{12}$ year.

Example 1

6 months = $\frac{1}{2}$ year   ⟨ 6 ⟩⟨ ÷ ⟩⟨ 12 ⟩⟨ = ⟩⟨   0 . 5 ⟩

Answer: **.5 year**

Example 2

1 year 8 months = $1\frac{8}{12}$ year ⟨ 8 ⟩⟨ ÷ ⟩⟨ 12 ⟩⟨ = ⟩⟨ 0 . 6 6 6 6 6 6 ⟩

Answer: **1.667 year**

= .667 ↑
part of the year rounded
to the thousandths place

A. Express each time below as a decimal. Round each decimal fraction to the thousandths place.

1. 5 months   **2.** 3 years 1 month   **3.** 4 years 7 months

B. Solve each problem below by using the interest formula. Round decimal fractions to the thousandths place before multiplying. Round each answer to the nearest cent.

1. How much interest would be earned on a deposit of $2,500 placed in a savings account for three years if the account pays 6% simple interest?

2. Larry borrowed $1,500 from his partner to buy stock. He agreed to repay the amount in 2 years, including 18% simple interest. At the end of two years, how much interest will he owe?

3. What amount of interest can Jules earn on $750 deposited for two years and three months in an account that pays 5.25% simple interest?

Questions 4–5 refer to the chart.

4. Doni deposited $375 in a new savings account at United Bank. How much will be in Doni's account at the end of 2 years 5 months?
(Hint: Total Saved = Principal + Interest)

5. Armand borrowed $650 from United Bank in order to buy a new TV set. Armand will repay the bank the entire amount at the end of 15 months. How much must Armand pay the bank at that time?
(Hint: Total Owed = Principal + Interest)

United Bank	
Simple Interest Accounts and Loans	
Savings Account	5.75%
IRA	6.82%
Car Loan	12.50%
Boat Loan	13.75%
Personal Loans	14.50%

PERCENT AND A FAMILY BUDGET

To keep track of expenses, many families prepare a household budget. Using a calculator makes it much easier to check and recheck numbers.

Last year the Corwin family had a take-home income of $14,624. At the end of the year, they prepared a record of their yearly expenses. Using this budget, the Corwins are better able to decide how to save money during the coming year.

The two circle graphs below show the Corwins' yearly expenses broken down into various expense categories.
- The graph at left shows the **dollar amount** spent in each category.
- The graph at right (partially completed) shows the **percent** of take-home income spent in each category.

The following example shows how the percent for housing (32%) is calculated.

Example

What percent of their take-home income do the Corwins spend on housing?

Step 1. On the graph at left, find the dollar amount for housing.
Answer: **$4,682**

Step 2. Calculate what percent $4,682 is of $14,624.

Press Keys: Display Reads:

(4)(6)(8)(2)(÷)(1)(4)(6)(2)(4)(%)*   (3 2 . 0 1 5 8 6 4)

Answer: **32%** (rounded to nearest %)

CORWIN FAMILY INCOME
Take-home Pay: $14,624

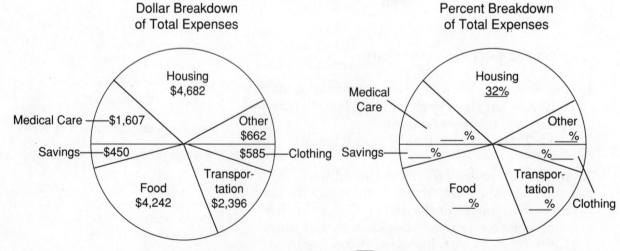

Dollar Breakdown of Total Expenses

Percent Breakdown of Total Expenses

Housing $4,682 / Medical Care —$1,607 / Other $662 / Savings—$450 / $585—Clothing / Food $4,242 / Transportation $2,396

Housing 32% / Medical Care / Other % / Savings— % / % / % Clothing / Food % / Transportation %

*On some calculators, you may need to press (=) to complete the calculation.

Use your calculator and the information on page 94 to do each problem below. Remember to use the percent circle (page 78) to help you decide whether to multiply or divide.

1. Fill in the Percent Breakdown of Total Expenses graph on page 94. Write the correct percent on each blank line. (The percent value for housing is completed as an example. Express each answer to the nearest percent.)

2. Last year Mrs. Corwin worked part-time and earned 16% of the family take-home income. What dollar amount of take-home income did Mrs. Corwin earn?

3. Each month last year, the Corwins made a $94.50 car payment. To the nearest percent, what percent of their yearly transportation costs was spent on car payments? (Hint: Don't forget to multiply monthly payment by the number of months in a year.)

4. The Corwins made monthly (12) rent payments of $285 during last year. To the nearest percent, what percent of their total take-home pay was spent last year for rent?

5. If the Corwins spent $78.45 last year on prescription drugs, what percent of their medical care expenses was spent for these medicines? Express your answer to the nearest percent.

6. Last year the Corwins donated 1.25% of their total take-home income to charity. To the nearest dollar, what amount did they give to charity?

7. To save money this year, the Corwins have decided to cut back on transportation costs. By taking the bus to work, Mr. Corwin figures he can save 15% on family transportation expenses. If he's right, how much money can Mr. Corwin actually save by riding the bus?

8. The Corwin family has set a goal of putting 25% more money into savings next year than they did last year. To achieve this goal, how much will they need to place in savings next year?

BRAIN TEASERS

You've now reached the end of the section on percent! If you like challenges, try the brain teasers on this page. They'll sharpen your thinking skills about calculators and percent problems.

Write

A. Match each question with the calculator solution that's used to answer that question. Write the letter of the calculator solution on the line to the left of each question.*

Question		Calculator Solution
_____ **1.** What is 18 + 15% of 18?	**a)**	(1)(5)(÷)(1)(8)(%)
_____ **2.** What percent of 18 is 15?	**b)**	(1)(8)(×)(1)(5)(%)
_____ **3.** 15% of what number is 18?	**c)**	(1)(8)(÷)(1)(5)(%)
_____ **4.** What is 18% of 15?	**d)**	(1)(8)(+)(1)(5)(%)
_____ **5.** What is 15% of 18?	**e)**	(1)(5)(×)(1)(8)(%)

Mental Calculation

B. See if you can guess what answer the calculator will display if you press each group of keys as shown below. **After you guess,** use your calculator to find the actual answer to each problem.*

		Guess	Actual
1. (1)(0)(0)(×)(1)(0)(0)(%)		_____	_____
2. (1)(0)(0)(×)(5)(0)(%)		_____	_____
3. (1)(0)(×)(5)(0)(%)		_____	_____
4. (1)(0)(0)(÷)(1)(0)(0)(%)		_____	_____
5. (1)(0)(0)(÷)(5)(0)(%)		_____	_____
6. (1)(0)(÷)(5)(0)(%)		_____	_____
7. (1)(0)(0)(+)(1)(0)(0)(%)		_____	_____
8. (1)(0)(0)(+)(5)(0)(%)		_____	_____
9. (1)(0)(+)(5)(0)(%)		_____	_____

* On some calculators, you may need to press (=) to complete the calculation.

PART 5

Using the Calculator's Memory

A **calculator memory** is a special place in a calculator where you can temporarily store a number. Until you erase this number or turn off your calculator, the stored number will remain in memory.

A calculator memory is **cumulative**. This means you can add to or subtract from a stored number as many times as you wish.

A calculator has a memory to give you an easy way to solve problems that involve more than one step.

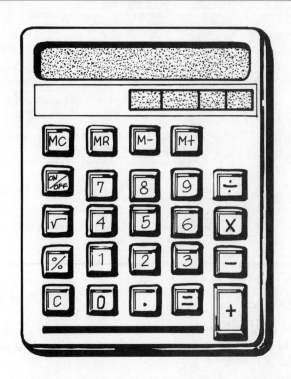

BECOMING FAMILIAR WITH YOUR CALCULATOR'S MEMORY

Using Memory Keys*

Most inexpensive calculators have the following memory keys:

$(M+)$, $(M-)$, (MR), (MC)

Uses of Memory Keys
$(M+)$ and $(M-)$ On most calculators, pressing either $(M+)$ or $(M-)$ completes a calculation and displays the answer—in the same way that pressing $(=)$ does. On others, you must press $(=)$. <ul><li>Pressing $(M+)$ also adds the displayed number to the memory.</li><li>Pressing $(M-)$ also subtracts the displayed number from the memory.</li></ul>
(MR) Memory Recall: Pressing (MR) displays the total currently stored in memory.
(MC) Memory Clear: Pressing (MC) clears (erases) the memory but not the display. (Some calculators combine the MR and MC functions on a single key. On these calculators, press the (MR/MC) key once to recall memory and twice to clear.)
*(Your calculator may not have these exact memory functions. If your keyboard is different, read your calculator's instruction booklet.)

Example 1

Add 15 to 12 and put the answer in the memory.

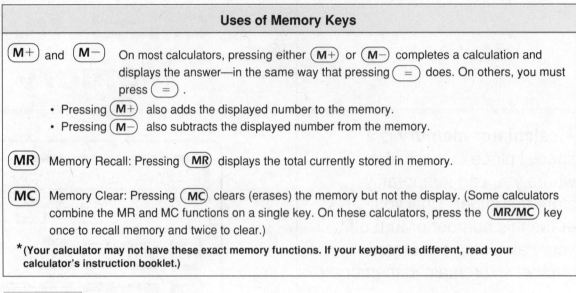

In the sequence shown at right, pressing $(M+)$:
* completes the addition of 15 + 12
* displays the answer 27, and
* stores the number 27 in the memory.

Press Keys	Display Reads
1 5	1 5.
+	1 5.
1 2*	1 2.
M+	2 7ᴹ number in memory

Pressing (C) (or other clear key) clears the display but not the memory.

| C | 0ᴹ |

Pressing (MR) displays the total (27) stored in memory.

| MR | 2 7ᴹ |

Pressing (MC) clears the memory, but not the display. The "M" disappears.

| MC | 2 7. |

> **Discovery**
>
> *The small "M" at the upper right of the display indicates that a number is stored in memory.*

In Example 1, you saw how $(M+)$ can be used to complete a calculation and to store the answer in memory. In Example 2, you see how a calculation can be done within the memory itself.

* On some calculators, you may need to press $(=)$ to complete the calculation before pressing $(M+)$.

Always clear **both** the memory **and** the display before starting a new problem. Before beginning Example 2:
- press (MC) once or (MR/MC) twice to clear memory
- press your clear key to clear the display

Example 2

Using memory keys only, subtract $36.89 and $19.95 from $87.75.

	Press Keys	Display Reads
Step 1. Enter 87.75 on the display. Press (M+) to place 87.75 in the memory.	8 7 · 7 5 (M+)	8 7 . 7 5 8 7 . 7 5 ᴹ
Step 2. Enter 36.89 on the display. Press (M−) to subtract 36.89 from the number (87.75) already stored in memory.	3 6 · 8 9 (M−)	3 6 . 8 9 ᴹ 3 6 . 8 9 ᴹ
Step 3. Enter 19.95 on the display. Press (M−) to subtract 19.95 from the number (87.75 − 36.89) already stored in the memory.	1 9 · 9 5 (M−)	1 9 . 9 5 ᴹ 1 9 . 9 5 ᴹ
Step 4. Press (MR) to display the new total (87.75 − 36.89 − 19.95) now in the memory.	(MR)	3 0 . 9 1 ᴹ

Answer: **$30.91**

*You may notice that both Examples 1 and 2 can easily be done without the use of memory keys. However, working with familiar problems here will help you gain confidence in the use of your calculator's memory.

Discovery

After pressing (M+) or (M−), you do not need to clear the display. The display clears automatically as you begin to enter the next number.

Write

Match each key with the function it performs. Write the letter of the function on the line to the left of the key symbol.

Keys	Key Functions
_____ 1. (M+)	**a.** Displays the total currently in memory.
_____ 2. (M−)	**b.** Clears the memory but not the display.
_____ 3. (MR)	**c.** Clears the display but not the memory.
_____ 4. (MC)	**d.** Subtracts the displayed number from the memory.
_____ 5. (C)	**e.** Adds the displayed number to the memory.

Memory keys are used to simplify many types of multistep word problems. To keep track of answers to each step of a problem, you can use memory keys instead of pencil and paper.

Take another look at an example.

Example

Ellen is buying six bottles of hair conditioner on sale. Each bottle costs $2.89. How much change will Ellen receive if she pays the clerk with a $20.00 bill?

Instead of solving this example in two steps, we can write the solution as a single expression, called an **arithmetic expression.**

Change = $20.00 − ($2.89 × 6)

total cost of
conditioner

- An **arithmetic expression** consists of numbers, products, and quotients combined by plus and minus signs.

- The solution steps for any multistep word problem can be written as an arithmetic expression.

You'll soon see how your calculator can help you quickly find the value of arithmetic expressions. First, though, it's a good idea to make sure you understand what arithmetic expressions mean.

EVALUATING ARITHMETIC EXPRESSIONS

- Multiply or divide numbers within parentheses before adding or subtracting numbers standing alone.

Arithmetic Expressions	Meaning
(19 + 11) − 7	Add 19 and 11; then subtract 7.
(15 × 6) − 13	Multiply 15 × 6; then subtract 13.
(125 ÷ 9) + 14	Divide 125 by 9; then add 14.
75 + (13 × 9)	Multiply 13 × 9; then add 75.
93 − (48 ÷ 12)	Divide 48 by 12; then subtract this quotient from 93.
(9 × 7) + (11 × 6)	Add the product of 9 × 7 to the product of 11 × 6.
(8 × 5) − (4 × 3)	Subtract the product of 4 × 3 from the product of 8 × 5.

- Always do addition or subtraction within parentheses first. Then multiply or divide. A number in front of the parentheses indicates multiplication.

Arithmetic Expressions	Meaning
7(8 + 4)	Add 8 and 4; then multiply the sum by 7.
9(6 − 3)	Subtract 3 from 6; then multiply the difference by 9.
(16 − 7) ÷ 5	Subtract 7 from 16; then divide this difference by 5.

Write

Complete the "Meaning" column for each arithmetic expression.

Arithmetic Expressions   **Meaning**

1. (26 + 14) − 9   Add __26__ and __14__; then subtract __9__.

2. (13 × 4) − 18   Multiply ____ × ____; then subtract ____.

3. (64 ÷ 8) + 11   Divide ____ by ____; then add ____.

4. 21 + (9 × 8)   Multiply ____ × ____; then add ____.

5. 60 − (56 ÷ 7)   Divide ____ by ____; then subtract this quotient from ____.

6. (7 × 6) + (8 × 3)   Add the product of ____ × ____ to the product of ____ × ____.

7. (9 × 8) − (7 × 6)   Subtract the product of ____ × ____ from the product of ____ × ____.

8. 9(7 + 6)   Add ____ and ____; then multiply the sum by ____.

9. 8(12 − 10)   Subtract ____ from ____; then multiply the difference by ____.

10. (30 − 12) ÷ 6   Subtract ____ from ____; then divide the difference by ____.

Expressions Involving Only Addition and Subtraction

- When only addition and subtraction are involved, press keys in the order of the steps given.

Example 1

Find the value of the following expression:

$57 + 19 - 26$

You do not need to use memory keys to solve this type of problem.

Answer: **50**

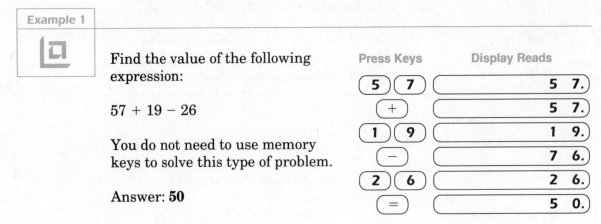

Press Keys	Display Reads
5 7	5 7.
+	5 7.
1 9	1 9.
−	7 6.
2 6	2 6.
=	5 0.

Expressions Involving Sums or Differences in Parentheses

- When an operation appears in parentheses, evaluate that sum or difference first. Then multiply or divide.

Example 2

Find the value of this expression:

$15 (23 - 7)$

As shown, first find the difference $23 - 7$, then multiply the difference by 15.

Pressing keys in this order ensures that you subtract before you multiply.

Answer: **240**

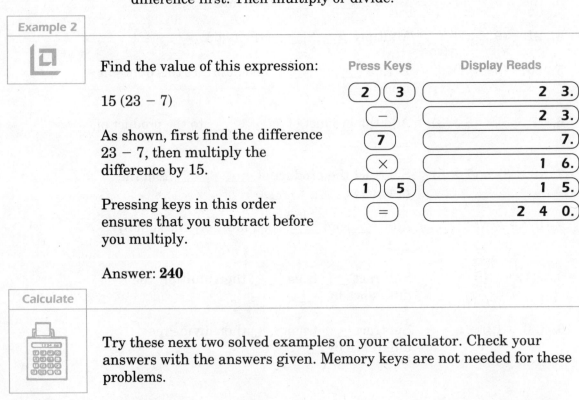

Press Keys	Display Reads
2 3	2 3.
−	2 3.
7	7.
×	1 6.
1 5	1 5.
=	2 4 0.

Calculate

Try these next two solved examples on your calculator. Check your answers with the answers given. Memory keys are not needed for these problems.

1. Evaluate $25 (56 - 29)$

Press keys: 5 6 − 2 9 × 2 5 =

Answer: **675**

2. Evaluate $(127 - 83) \div 11$

Press keys: (1)(2)(7)(−)(8)(3)(÷)(1)(1)(=)

Answer: **4**

Expressions Involving Separated Terms

Terms are numbers, products, and quotients. **Separated terms** have plus $(+)$ or minus $(-)$ signs between them.
 • Individually add (or subtract) each term to (or from) the memory.

Example 3

Evaluate $275 - (13 \times 9)$

	Press Keys	Display Reads
Step 1. Place the whole number 275 in the memory. Press keys: (2)(7)(5)(M+)	(2)(7)(5) (M+)	2 7 5 . 2 7 5 ᴹ
Step 2. Subtract the product 13×9 from the memory. Press keys: (1)(3)(×)(9)(M−)	(1)(3) (×) (9) * (M−)	1 3 ᴹ 1 3 ᴹ 9 ᴹ 1 1 7 ᴹ
Note: Pressing (M−) completes the calculation **and** subtracts the product from the memory.		
Step 3. Press (MR) to display the answer—the total now stored in memory.	(MR)	1 5 8 ᴹ

Answer: **158**

Calculate

Try these next two solved problems on your calculator. Check your answers with the answers given. Be sure to clear the memory **and** the display between each problem.

1. Evaluate $(35 \div 8) + 16.75$

Press keys: (3)(5)(÷)(8)*(M+)(1)(6)(.)(7)(5)(M+)(MR)

Answer: **21.125**

2. Evaluate $(24 \times 19) + (13 \times 12)$

Press keys: (2)(4)(×)(1)(9)*(M+)(1)(3)(×)(1)(2)*(M+)(MR)

Answer: **612**

* On some calculators, you may need to press (=) before (M+) or (M−).

GAINING CONFIDENCE WITH ARITHMETIC EXPRESSIONS

On the previous two pages, we've shown how a calculator can be used to find the value of arithmetic expressions. Now on this page and the next are calculator exercises designed to help you gain confidence in this newly learned skill.

Calculate

Find the value of each arithmetic expression below. The correct keying and the answer are shown for the first problem in each group of expressions.

A. Expressions involving only addition and subtraction
- Press keys in order of steps given. Memory keys are not used.

1. 28 − 17 + 14
   ②⑧⊖①⑦⊕①④⊜
   Answer: **25**

2. $12.43 + $9.36 − $4.06

3. 396 − 209 − 43 + 37

4. 207 + 111 − 73 − 61

5. $13.46 − $2.09 − $3.12

6. $4.25 − $2.19 − $1.18 + $.24

B. Expressions involving parentheses
- Evaluate the sum or difference within the parentheses first. Then multiply or divide as indicated. Memory keys are not used.

1. 12(43 + 7)
   ④③⊕⑦⊗①②⊜
   Answer: **600**

2. (56 − 28) ÷ 4

3. ($4.56 + $2.31) × 3

4. (45 + 28 − 19) ÷ 9

5. 14(63 − 35)

6. (29 − 13) × 5

7. ($6.25 + $2.85) ÷ 2

8. (112 + 109 + 121) ÷ 3

C. Expressions involving separated products and quotients

- Individually add (or subtract) each whole number, product, or quotient to (or from) the memory.

  Remember: Clear the memory and the display as you begin a new problem.

1. $156 + (18 \times 3)$

    ①⑤⑥Ⓜ➕①⑧✕③⃰Ⓜ➕ⓂⓡR

    Answer: **210**

2. $9 + (104 \div 13)$

3. $18.7 + (4.2 \times 3)$

4. $(7.2 \times 6) + (3.4 \times 7)$

5. $(84 \times 3) - (57 \times 2)$

6. $37 - (3 \times 4)$

7. $15 - (153 \div 17)$

8. $27.6 - (7.8 \times 2)$

9. $(\$3.79 \times 4) + (\$2.87 \times 5)$

10. $\$50.00 - (\$13.49 \times 2) - (\$5.88 \times 3)$

D. Mixed practice

1. $\$7.56 + \$2.89 - \$3.57$

2. $5(\$8.29 - \$6.42)$

3. $(\$2.49 \times 3) + (\$5.18 \times 2)$

4. $\$10.00 - \$2.99 - \$1.89$

5. $3(143 + 231)$

6. $(5.7 + 3.6) \times 7$

7. $(\$27.46 - \$17.32) \div 2$

8. $(\$14.68 + \$16.20 + \$12.44) \div 3$

9. $(\$5.89 - \$2.99) \times 4$

10. $\$25.00 - (\$5.25 \times 3) + (\$4.89 \times 2)$

---

* On some calculators, you may need to press ⭕= before Ⓜ➕ or Ⓜ➖.

CALCULATOR POWER IN MULTISTEP WORD PROBLEMS

The first step in using the full power of your calculator to solve a multistep word problem is to write the solution as an arithmetic expression.

Example 1

Lex brought 196 colored markers to school. He gave 84 markers to students in his morning class. He divided the rest equally among the 16 students in his afternoon class. How many markers did each student in the afternoon class get?

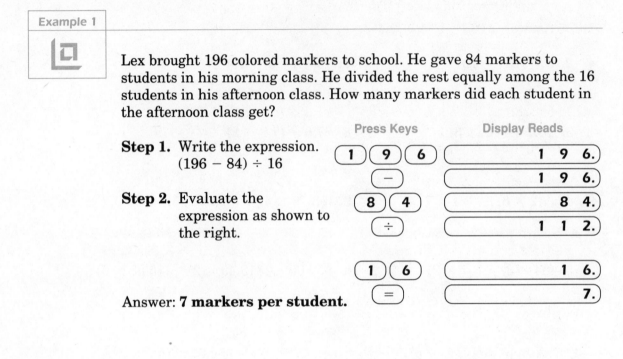

Step 1. Write the expression.
$(196 - 84) \div 16$

Step 2. Evaluate the expression as shown to the right.

Answer: **7 markers per student.**

Example 2

Kara bought 3 new blouses at a cost of $18.99 each. The store will allow her to pay with a check for more than the total so she can have cab fare home. If she pays with a check for $66.00, how much change will she receive?

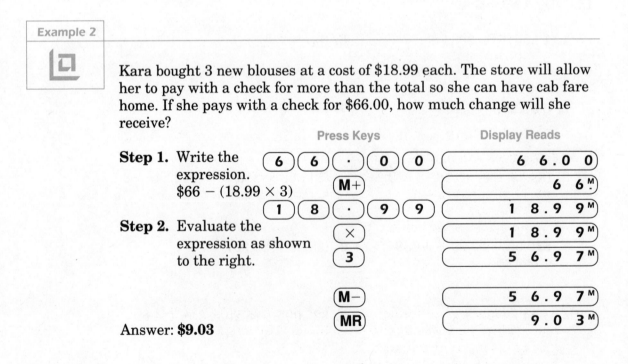

Step 1. Write the expression.
$\$66 - (18.99 \times 3)$

Step 2. Evaluate the expression as shown to the right.

Answer: **$9.03**

A. Circle the one arithmetic expression that will give the correct answer to each problem. Then use your calculator to evaluate that expression.

1. Sean gave the clerk $25.00 to pay for a $14.79 pillow and a $4.99 pillowcase. How much change should Sean receive?

    a) $25.00 − $14.79 + $4.99
    b) $25.00 − $14.79 − $4.99
    c) $14.79 + $4.99 − $25.00

2. Bill and two friends agreed to split the $3.95 rental cost of a VCR and two movies, each movie renting for $1.99. To the nearest cent, what is Bill's share of the total cost?

    a) ($3.95 + $1.99) ÷ 3
    b) ($3.95 − $1.99 − $1.99) ÷ 3
    c) ($3.95 + $1.99 + $1.99) ÷ 3

3. Before writing a check for $41.49 and making an $85.00 deposit, Manuel had a checking balance of $152.90. What is his new balance?

    a) $152.90 − $41.49 − $85.00
    b) $152.90 + $41.49 − $85.00
    c) $152.90 − $41.49 + $85.00

4. The eight employees of Jamie's collected $334.80 in tips last week. Jamie keeps the first $50.00 and splits the rest equally among his eight employees. How much did each employee receive in tips last week?

    a) ($334.80 + $50.00) ÷ 8
    b) ($334.80 − $50.00) ÷ 8
    c) ($334.80 − $50.00) ÷ 9

5. Jeb's truck can haul 11.5 cubic yards of dirt per load. Jeb was able to haul 8 full loads on Saturday and 9 full loads on Sunday. How many cubic yards of dirt did Jeb haul on these two days?

    a) (9 + 8) × 11.5
    b) (9 − 8) × 11.5
    c) (9 + 8) ÷ 11.5

6. Every Monday, Wednesday, and Friday, Jake jogs 5 miles during his morning workout. Each Tuesday and Thursday he jogs 3 miles. How many total miles does Jake jog each week?

    a) (3 + 2) × 8
    b) (3 × 5) + (2 × 3)
    c) (5 + 3) × 5

B. Write an arithmetic expression that shows how to solve each problem below. Then use your calculator to find the value of each expression you've written.

1. Before writing a check for $18.75 and making a deposit of $125.94, Judy had $84.29 in her checking account. What is the new balance in her account?

   expression: _____

   value: _____

2. After writing a check for $51.38 and making a deposit of $53.00, Erik's checking balance is $241.85. Determine Erik's balance **before** these transactions.

   expression: _____

   value: _____

3. Vince walks to work and back each day, five days per week. If he lives 1.9 miles from work, how many miles does Vince walk each week going to and from work?

   expression: _____

   value: _____

4. How much lighter than 20 pounds is a group of four packages if each package weighs 4.3 pounds?

   expression: _____

   value: _____

5. Cora bought a new clothes dryer for $329.99. She made a down payment of $44.99 and agreed to pay off the balance in 3 equal monthly payments. If she pays no interest, how much will Cora pay each month?

   expression: _____

   value: _____

6. For Christmas, Del bought 4.5 pounds of chicken priced at $1.08 per pound and 6.4 pounds of beef priced at $1.75 per pound. How much more did Del pay for the beef than he paid for the chicken?

   expression: _____

   value: _____

7. During league play Saturday, Julie bowled games of 182, 175, and 193. To the nearest whole number, what was Julie's average score that evening?

   expression: _____

   value: _____

SPECIAL MULTISTEP PROBLEM: FINDING PERCENT INCREASE OR DECREASE

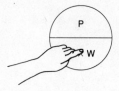

One type of multistep problem involves finding percent increase or percent decrease. These problems combine your percent skills with your skills of evaluating arithmetic expressions.

$$\% = \frac{P}{W} = \frac{\text{part (amount of increase)}}{\text{original amount}}$$

Example

When she changed jobs, Lee's monthly salary rose from $720 to $864. What percent salary increase is this?

Step 1. Subtract to find the **amount of increase**—the part (*P*).
$P = \$864 - \$720$

Step 2. Divide *P* by *W* (the original amount $720) to find the **percent increase** (%).

$$\% = \frac{P}{W} = \frac{\$864 - \$720}{\$720}$$

$$\% = (\$864 - \$720) \div \$720$$

To evaluate the expression for %, press keys as shown at right.

Press Keys	Display Reads
8 6 4	8 6 4.
−	8 6 4.
7 2 0	7 2 0.
÷	1 4 4.
7 2 0	7 2 0.
% *	2 0.

Answer: **20%**

Calculate

Calculate each percent increase and percent decrease below.

A. 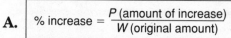 % increase = $\dfrac{P\text{ (amount of increase)}}{W\text{ (original amount)}}$

B. 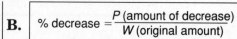 % decrease = $\dfrac{P\text{ (amount of decrease)}}{W\text{ (original amount)}}$

A.
1. Last month, Cybil's salary was raised from $5.60 per hour to $6.30 per hour. What percent raise did Cybil receive?
2. Between 1986 and 1990, the value of Will's house increased from $48,600 to $62,800. To the nearest percent, what percent value increase is this?
3. Between September 1st and June 1st, the average weekly rainfall in Newton increased from 1.2 inches to 1.5 inches. What percent increase in rainfall does this change represent?

B.
1. Nora's reduced the price of a wool sweater from $38.50 to $27.95. To the nearest percent, what percent price reduction is this?
2. Between 1980 and 1990, the population of Oak Grove decreased from 72,600 to 61,710. What percent population decrease does this change represent?
3. For the weekend, Jerry's lowered the price of its single-scoop ice cream cones from $1.25 to $.75. What percent price decrease is this price reduction?

* On some calculators, you may need to press = to complete the calculation.

PART 6

Algebra and geometry may seem intimidating because of the number of complex calculations. On the next few pages, you will see how a calculator can simplify many types of problems.

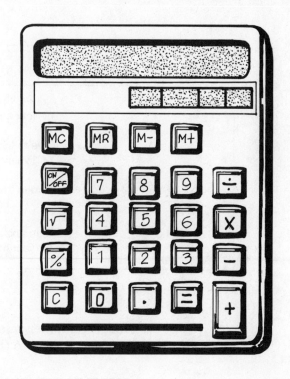

A **power** is the product of a number multiplied by itself one or more times. For example, "two to the third power" means "$2 \times 2 \times 2$."

In symbols, we usually write a power as a **base** and an **exponent.**

$$2 \times 2 \times 2 = 2^3 \leftarrow \text{exponent}$$

$$\uparrow \text{— base}$$

The **exponent**, 3, tells how many times the **base**, 2, must be multiplied by itself.

- To find the value of a number with an exponent, multiply the base as many times as you see the exponent

$$2^3 = \boxed{2} \boxed{\times} \boxed{2} \boxed{\times} \boxed{2} \boxed{=} \boxed{\qquad\qquad 8.}$$

Base and Exponent	In Words	Meaning	Value
4^2	"four to the second power" or "four squared" *	4×4	16
5^3	"five to the third power" or "five cubed" *	$5 \times 5 \times 5$	125
2^4	"two to the fourth power"	$2 \times 2 \times 2 \times 2$	16
1.3^4	"one and three tenths to the fourth power"	$1.3 \times 1.3 \times 1.3 \times 1.3$	2.8561

*Note: A number raised to the second power is often said to be "squared." A number raised to the third power is often said to be "cubed."

Because powers involve many multiplications, your calculator is very useful in finding the value of a power.

Example

Using your calculator, find the value of 2.4^3.

To find the value of 2.4^3, multiply $2.4 \times 2.4 \times 2.4$.

Answer: **13.824**

Press Keys	Display Reads
$\boxed{2}\boxed{\cdot}\boxed{4}$	2.4
$\boxed{\times}$	2.4
$\boxed{2}\boxed{\cdot}\boxed{4}$	2.4
$\boxed{\times}$	5.76
$\boxed{2}\boxed{\cdot}\boxed{4}$	2.4
$\boxed{=}$	13.824

Calculate each value below. Either enter the number each time or use the multiplication constant feature on your calculator. To do this, read the **Discovery** below.

1. 4^2 0.4^2 4.1^2 8^2 12^2

2. 5^3 6^4 2^3 8^3 9^4

3. 3.4^2 6.7^4 9.2^2 6.8^3 7.2^4

4. 8^4 4.6^3 7^4 3^3 3.4^4

Discovery

*Most calculators have a **multiplication constant** feature. This feature simplifies the keying you do to find the value of a power. Instead of pressing the number and the ⊗ key repeatedly, you only press the ⊜ key repeatedly.*

The following examples will show both ways to find the value of a power.

Power	Familiar Multiplication	Multiplication Constant
7^2	7 × 7 =	7 × =
7^3	7 × 7 × 7 =	7 × = =
7^4	7 × 7 × 7 × 7 =	7 × = = =

After entering 7 × ,

- *Pressing* ⊜ *once gives the value of 7 to the second power.*
- *Pressing* ⊜ *twice gives the value of 7 to the third power.*
- *Pressing* ⊜ *three times gives the value of 7 to the fourth power.*

To see if you have this feature on your calculator (you probably do), try finding the values of the powers given as examples in the box on page 112.

The **square root** of a number is found by asking, "What number times itself equals this number?" For example, to find the square root of 36 you ask, "What number times itself equals 36?"

The answer is 6 because $6 \times 6 = 36$. The number 6 is the square root of 36.

The symbol for square root is $\sqrt{}$. For example, $\sqrt{36} = 6$.

Numbers that have whole number square roots are called **perfect squares.** A list of perfect squares is easily made by "squaring" whole numbers. The first 12 perfect squares are shown in the table below.

Table of Perfect Squares			
$1^2 = 1$	$4^2 = 16$	$7^2 = 49$	$10^2 = 100$
$2^2 = 4$	$5^2 = 25$	$8^2 = 64$	$11^2 = 121$
$3^2 = 9$	$6^2 = 36$	$9^2 = 81$	$12^2 = 144$

Your calculator is equipped with a square root key $\sqrt{}$ or $\sqrt{x}$. The square root key enables you to easily find the square root of **any** number, not just perfect squares.

Example

What is the square root of 17?

To solve on your calculator, enter the number 17, then press the square root key.

Press Keys — Display Reads

`1` `7` — `1 7.`
`√` — `4 . 1 2 3 1 0 5 6`

Answer: **4.12** (rounded to the hundredths place)

Write

A. Write each sentence below in symbols. The first one is completed as an example.

1. 8 is the square root of 64. $\underline{8 = \sqrt{64}}$

2. 13 is the square root of 169. _____

3. 2.4 is the square root of 5.76. _____

Calculate

B. Use your calculator to find each square root below. Round decimal fractions to the hundredths place.

1. $\sqrt{225}$ $\sqrt{400}$ $\sqrt{900}$ $\sqrt{10}$ $\sqrt{20}$

2. $\sqrt{23}$ $\sqrt{42}$ $\sqrt{15.6025}$ $\sqrt{0.746}$ $\sqrt{0.09}$

Evaluating Expressions Containing Squares and Square Roots

In some problems, squares and square roots appear together. On this page, we'll show how the use of memory keys can simplify finding the values of such expressions.

Example

Find the value of $\sqrt{11^2 + 13^2}$.

To evaluate this expression, you must first find the value of the sum of the two squares. You then find the square root of this sum.

	Press Keys	Display Reads

Step 1. Compute the value 11^2. Press **M+** to place this value in memory.

$\boxed{1}\ \boxed{1}\ \boxed{\times}\ \boxed{1}\ \boxed{1}\ \boxed{M+}$ $1\ 2\ 1\ ^{M}$

Step 2. Compute the value 13^2. Press **M+** to add this value to the number (11^2) now stored in memory. (You would use **M−** for a problem involving subtraction.)

$\boxed{1}\ \boxed{3}\ \boxed{\times}\ \boxed{1}\ \boxed{3}\ \boxed{M+}$ $1\ 6\ 9\ ^{M}$

Step 3. Press **MR** to display the sum $11^2 + 13^2$ now stored in memory.

$\boxed{MR}$ $2\ 9\ 0\ ^{M}$

Step 4.
Press $\sqrt{}$ (or $\sqrt{x}$) to find the square root of 290.

$\boxed{\sqrt{}}$ $1\ 7\ .\ 0\ 2\ 9\ 3\ 8\ 6\ ^{M}$

Answer: **17.03** (rounded to 100ths place)

Calculate

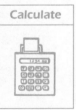

Calculate the value of each expression below. Round each answer to the hundredths place. Remember to clear the display and the memory before you start each problem.

1. $8^2 + 9^2$ $4.5^2 + 6.8^2$ $12^2 - 7^2$

2. $\sqrt{3^2 + 4^2}$ $\sqrt{8^2 + 11^2}$ $\sqrt{92^2 - 8^2}$

3. $\sqrt{14^2 + 17^2}$ $\sqrt{6.7^2 + 4.2^2}$ $\sqrt{92^2 - 82^2}$

* On some calculators, you may need to press $\boxed{=}$ before **M+**.

TOPIC 3: RIGHT TRIANGLES AND THE PYTHAGOREAN THEOREM

On these next two pages, you'll see how memory keys can simplify problems involving the **Pythagorean Theorem.** First, a short review.

A **right triangle** is a triangle in which two sides meet at a right angle. The side opposite the right angle is called the **hypotenuse.**

The Greek mathematician Pythagoras discovered that the square of the length of the hypotenuse of a right triangle is equal to the sum of the squares of the lengths of the other two sides. This relationship is called the Pythagorean Theorem.

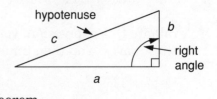

Using the labels on the triangle above, the Pythagorean Theorem is written as:

$$c^2 = a^2 + b^2$$

In other words, hypotenuse squared = side squared + side squared.

Example

What is the length of the hypotenuse (c) of the triangle pictured at right?

From the Pythagorean Theorem, we can write:

$$c^2 = 7^2 + 9^2$$

You can find c by taking the square root of the sum of the squares of the sides.

$$c = \sqrt{7^2 + 9^2}$$

To solve for c on your calculator, follow the steps shown below.

	Press Keys	Display Reads
Step 1. Compute 7^2. Place the answer (49) in memory.	7 $\times$ 7 *$M+$	$4\ 9$ M
Step 2. Compute 9^2. Add this answer (81) to the memory.	9 $\times$ 9 *$M+$	$8\ 1$ M
Step 3. Press MR to display the sum of $7^2 + 9^2$ (49 + 81).	MR	$1\ 3\ 0$ M
Step 4. As displayed, this sum is 130. Press $\sqrt{\ }$ (or $\sqrt{x}$) to find the square root of 130.	$\sqrt{\ }$	$1\ 1.4\ 0\ 1\ 7\ 5\ 4$ M

Answer: **11.4 in.** (rounded to 10ths place)

* On some calculators, you may need to press $=$ before $M+$.

A. Fill in the key symbols below to show how to compute the length of the hypotenuse of the right triangle shown at right. **Do not solve the problem.**

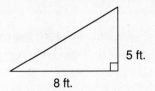

5 ft.

8 ft.

Step 1. Compute 5^2. Place the anwer in memory.

Step 2. Compute 8^2. Add this number to the memory.

Step 3. Display the sum $5^2 + 8^2$, the sum that is now stored in memory.

Step 4. Find the square root of the displayed number (the sum of $5^2 + 8^2$).

Press Keys

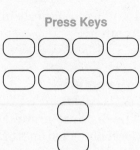

Calculate

B. Using your calculator, solve each problem below.

1. In a right triangle, one side measures 7 feet, and the second side measures 10 feet. To the nearest tenth of a foot, what is the length of the hypotenuse of this triangle?

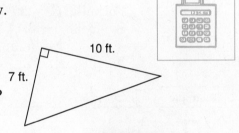

10 ft.

7 ft.

2. A ladder is leaning against the side of a house. The base of the ladder is 5 feet from the house. The top of the ladder just reaches the roof that is 13 feet above the ground. Determine the length of the ladder to the nearest 10th foot.

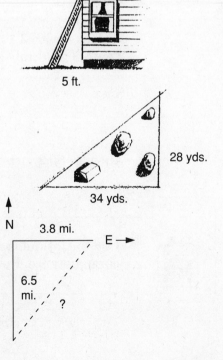

13 ft. high

5 ft.

3. One side of a triangular lot measures 28 yards long. A second side measures 34 yards long. To the nearest yard, what is the length of the third side of this lot?

28 yds.

34 yds.

4. Alissa hiked 6.5 miles due north of her car before turning east. She then walked 3.8 miles due east before stopping to rest. At the point she rested, what was Alissa's direct distance from her car? Express your answer to the nearest tenth mile.

N

3.8 mi.

E →

6.5 mi.

?

TOPIC 4: WORKING WITH MEASUREMENT FORMULAS

A **measurement formula** is a rule written in symbols. To find a perimeter, an area, or a volume, substitute numbers for symbols and do the arithmetic.

In a formula, multiplication is indicated by placing one symbol next to another.

Perimeter

The distance around a flat (plane) object is known as its **perimeter.** The symbol for perimeter is P. Perimeter is measured in units of length.

- Perimeter of a rectangle
  Formula: $P = 2(l + w)$
  Symbols: l = length
  $\quad\quad\quad w$ = width

A **square** has 4 equal sides. The perimeter of a square is given by the formula $P = 4s$, where s is the length of each side.

- Circumference of a circle
  Formula: $C = 2\pi r$
  Symbols: $\pi \approx 3.14$
  $\quad\quad\quad r$ = radius

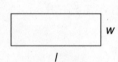

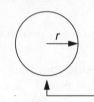

circumference (perimeter of a circle)

Example

Find the circumference of a circle with an 8-inch radius. Round the answer to the nearest tenth inch.

In the formula $C = 2\pi r$, replace π with 3.14 and r with 8. Multiply as shown at right.

$C = 2\pi r$
$\quad = 2 \times 3.14 \times 8$

Answer: **50.2 inches**

Press Keys	Display Reads
2	2.
×	2.
3 . 1 4	3.1 4
×	6.2 8
8	8.
=	5 0.2 4

Calculate

Use the formulas above and your calculator to find each perimeter and circumference. Round each answer to the nearest 10th unit.

1.

4.1875 in.

4.1875 in.

2.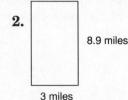

8.9 miles

3 miles

3.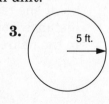

5 ft.

Area is a measure of surface. Area is measured in square units such as square inches, square feet, square yards, etc. The symbol for area is A.

- Area of a triangle
  Formula: $A = \frac{1}{2}bh$
  Symbols: b = base
  $\quad\quad\quad h$ = height

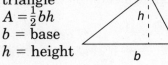

This formula can also be written as $A = (bh) \div 2$ which means $A = b \times h \div 2$. Use this version when using your calculator to find the area of a triangle.

- Area of a rectangle
  Formula: $A = lw$
  Symbols: l = length
  $\quad\quad\quad w$ = width

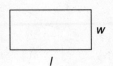

The area of a **square** is given by the formula $A = s^2$, where s is the length of each side.

- Area of a circle
  Formula: $A = \pi r^2$
  Symbols: $\pi \approx 3.14$
  $\quad\quad\quad r$ = radius

Example

Find the area of a circle with an eight-inch radius. Round the answer to the nearest tenth square inch.

In the area formula, replace π with 3.14 and r with 8. Using your calculator, multiply as shown at right.

$A = \pi r^2$
$\quad = \pi \times r \times r$
$\quad = 3.14 \times 8 \times 8$

Answer: 201 square inches

Press Keys	Display Reads
3 · 1 4	3.14
×	3.14
8	8.
×	25.12
8	8.
=	200.96

Calculate

Use the formulas and your calculator to find each area below. Round to the nearest tenth square unit.

1.
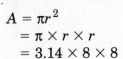
1.9 ft.
4.6 ft.

2.
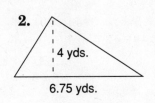
4 yds.
6.75 yds.

3.
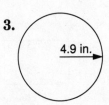
4.9 in.

Volume

Volume is a measure of space. Volume can refer to the space taken up by a solid object, or volume can refer to the space enclosed by the surface of a solid figure. The symbol for volume is V. Volume is measured in cubic units such as cubic inches, cubic feet, cubic yards, etc.

- Volume of a rectangular solid
  Formula: $V = lwh$
  Symbols: l = length
  w = width
  h = height

A **cube** is a rectangular solid in which $l = w = h$. The volume of a cube is given by the formula $V = s^3$, where s is the length of each side.

- Volume of a cylinder
  Formula: $V = \pi r^2 h$
  Symbols: $\pi \approx 3.14$
  r = radius
  h = height

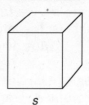

Example

What is the volume of a cylinder that has a radius of 1.5 feet and a height of 4.5 feet? Express your answer to the nearest tenth cubic foot.

In the volume formula, replace π by 3.14, r by 1.5, and h by 4.5.

$$V = \pi r^2 h$$
$$= \pi \times r \times r \times h$$
$$= 3.14 \times 1.5 \times 1.5 \times 4.5$$

Answer: **31.8 cubic feet.**

Press Keys	Display Reads
3 . 1 4	3 . 1 4
×	3 . 1 4
1 . 5	1 . 5
×	4 . 7 1
1 . 5	1 . 5
×	7 . 0 6 5
4 . 5	4 . 5
=	3 1 . 7 9 2 5

Calculate

Use the formulas above and your calculator to find the volumes below. Express each answer to the nearest cubic unit.

1.

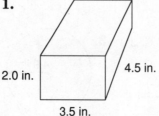

2.0 in.   4.5 in.   3.5 in.

2.

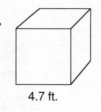

4.7 ft.

3.

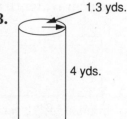

1.3 yds.   4 yds.

CALCULATOR POWER IN MEASUREMENT WORD PROBLEMS

Calculate

Write the formula that applies in each problem below. Then use your calculator to find each value asked for.

1. Hank wants to put a piece of weather stripping completely around the front door of his house. What is the minimum amount of stripping Hank will need if his door is 6.5 feet high and 2.9 feet wide?

   Formula: Answer:

2. The circular wading pool in Central Park has a radius of 14 feet. To the nearest foot, what is the distance around this pool?

   Formula: Answer:

3. To the nearest square foot, what is the area of the wading pool described in question 2?

   Formula: Answer:

4. A triangular piece of glass measures four feet across the base and is three feet high. How many square feet of glass are contained in this piece?

   Formula: Answer:

5. The rectangular field behind Joe Miller's barn measures 73 yards long and 46 yards wide. Determine the area of this field.

   Formula: Answer:

6. How many cubic feet of water does a water mattress hold if the mattress is six feet long, five feet wide, and six inches thick? (Hint: Change 6 inches to a decimal fraction part of a foot before multiplying to find volume.)

   Formula: Answer:

7. What volume of water can a cylindrical water tower hold if the tower measures 18 feet high and has a radius of 15 feet? Express your answer to the nearest cubic foot.

   Formula: Answer:

When you deposit money in a savings account, banks pay a form of interest called **compound interest.** This is how it works.

> At the end of a short period, called the **compounding period,** the bank pays you simple interest. That interest is then added to the principal. During the next compounding period, the added interest also earns interest. The total interest earned is called **compound interest.** With compound interest, interest earns interest!

To find the total value of your balance at any particular time, the bank uses the **compound interest formula:**

$$A = P\left(1 + \frac{R}{m}\right)^n$$

A = Accumulated amount: original principal plus all interest
P = Original principal
R = Yearly percent rate
m = Number of compounding periods per year that interest is paid
n = Total number of times that interest is paid
    (m times the number of years)

Example

$2,000 is placed in a savings account for one year. The account pays 5% interest, compounded every three months. What will be the balance at the end of the year?

Step 1. Identify P, R, m, and n.
    (Write R as a decimal.)
- P and R are given. $P = \$2,000$ $R = 5\% = .05$
- To find m, divide 1 year (12 months) by the compounding period, 3 months. $m = \frac{12}{3} = 4$
- To find n, multiply m by the number of years:
  $n = 4 \times 1 = 4$

Step 2. Substitute the values of P, R, m, and n into the formula for A.
$$A = 2,000\left(1 + \frac{.05}{4}\right)^4$$

Step 3. Calculate the value of A as follows:
- Evaluate $1 + \frac{.05}{4}$
- Use the multiplication constant (page 113) to find the value of $(1.0125)^4$
- Multiply by 2,000.

Press Keys	Display Reads
. 0 5 ÷ 4 + 1 =	1.0125
× = = =	1.0509452
× 2 0 0 0 =	2101.8904

Answer: **$2,101.89**

Complete the steps needed to solve each problem below.

1. Jenny placed \$4,500 in a savings account that earns 6% interest. If the interest is compounded every four months, what will be Jenny's total balance at the end of one year?

   Step 1. Identify P, R, m, and n.

   $P = \$4,500 \qquad R = 6\% = .06$

   $m = \frac{12}{4} = 3 \qquad n = 3 \times 1 = 3$

   Step 2. Substitute these values into the formula for A.

   $A = 4,500 \left(1 + \frac{.06}{3}\right)^{3}$

   Step 3. Calculate the value of A.
   - Evaluate $1 + \frac{.06}{3}$
   - Press $\boxed{\times}\,\boxed{=}\,\boxed{=}$
   - Multiply by 4,500

2. If \$2,750 is invested and earns 14% interest, compounded every 6 months, how much will the investment be worth in 18 months? (Think of 18 months as 1.5 years.)

   Step 1. Identify P, R, m, and n.

   $P = \$2,750 \qquad R = 14\% = .14$

   $m = \frac{12}{6} = 2 \qquad n = 2 \times 1.5 = 3$

   Step 2. Substitute these values into the formula for A.

   $A = P\left(1 + \frac{R}{m}\right)^{n}$

   Step 3. Calculate the value of A.
   - Evaluate . . . .
   - Press . . .
   - Multiply by . . .

3. James loaned his partner \$6,500 for a real estate deal. The partner promised to pay James 16% interest, compounded every six months. If James is repaid the total amount at the end of two years, how much money will he receive? (Use steps 1–3 as shown in the two problems above.)

Congratulations on completing *Calculator Power!* We hope you find your new skills valuable both at home and on the job.

These final three pages will give you a chance to review your calculator skills in some of the ways you're most likely to use them. Work each problem carefully with your calculator, and check your answers with those given on page 136.

Review indicated pages as needed.

Whole Numbers and Money (Review pages 9–46)

1. Determine the daily balance in the checking account register below. Record your answers in the BALANCE column.

RECORD ALL CHARGES OR CREDITS THAT AFFECT YOUR ACCOUNT

Number	Date	Description of Transaction	Payment/Debit (−)	T	Fee (If Any) (−)	Deposit/Credit (+)	Balance $	
							641	90
309	7/6	Hillcrest Apartments	$ 275 00		$	$		
310	7/7	Value Food Store	19 85					
311	7/10	Northern Power Co.	107 33					
312		— VOID —						
313	7/14	Hair Palace	12 00					
	7/16	Deposit Paycheck				342 61		
314	7/18	2D Variety Store	27 93					

REMEMBER TO RECORD AUTOMATIC PAYMENTS/DEPOSITS ON DATE AUTHORIZED

2. Complete the Total Amount column for items 2 through 5 on the purchase order form below. Then add the five entries to find the Total Purchase amount.

WHOLESALE BATHROOM SUPPLIES

	Item #	Description	Quantity	Cost/Per	Total Amount
1.	A 241	Bath mat	14	18.45	$258.30
2.	B 647	Bath towel	29	10.98	
3.	D 832	Wall mirror	7	73.49	
4.	F 301	Shower Curtain	16	19.99	
5.	P 970	Window Curtain	8	48.75	
				Total Purchase	

3. Which of the three stores below is offering the best buy on a case of 12 bottles of Hair Glow shampoo?

FOOD PLUS HAIR GLOW Shampoo	VALUE RITE HAIR GLOW Shampoo	DONNIE'S HAIR GLOW Shampoo
$1.89 per bottle $1.25 rebate each case	$1.79 per bottle $.14 per bottle discount on case purchase	$1.74 per bottle "Buy 11 and get 1 free!"

4. Darrell can carry 348 bricks each trip in his truck.

a) How many trips will it take Darrell to move 7,500 bricks from the brick yard to the construction site?

b) How many bricks will Darrell carry on his final trip?

Decimals (Review pages 47–76)

5. Cecelia's gas bills for a four month period are shown below. Compute Cecelia's average monthly gas bill during this time. Round your answer to the nearest $1.00.

November: $158.94
December: $183.56
January: $192.67
February: $174.40

6. On the scale below, fill in the $ PER LB. amount to show how much Doreen is paying per pound for the salmon she is buying.

SCALE	
Total Price	$ 32.47
6.52 LB.	$ __.__ ← Fill in this amount.
Weight	$ PER LB.

Questions 7–9 are based on the paycheck stub below.

SMYTHE ELECTRONICS

Employee: Angie Lewis	Gross Pay	Federal Income Tax	State Income Tax	Social Security	Net Pay
Current Pay Period (two weeks)	$576.94	$62.48	$11.14	$40.02	$463.30
Year-to-Date	$4,038.58	$437.36	$77.98	$280.14	$3.243.10

7. How much are Angie's total deductions for the pay period shown?

8. About how much federal income tax does Angie pay each year?

9. Angie works 40 hours each week. Determine to the nearest penny her

a) gross pay per hour
b) net pay per hour

Percents (Review pages 77–96)

Questions 10–12 refer to the circle graph shown at right.

10. What percent of their total take-home income do the Allisons spend on food?

ALLISON FAMILY INCOME
Take-home Pay: $16,804

Dollar Breakdown of Total Expenses

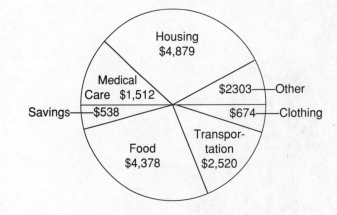

11. The Allisons spend 65% of their housing expenses on rent. To the nearest dollar, how much yearly rent do the Allisons pay?

12. Next year the Allisons plan to save 15% more money than they saved this year. To do this, how much will they need to save next year?

Using the Calculator's Memory (Review pages 97–109)

Questions 13 and 14 are based on the following information.

> For the barbeque, Adam bought 3.5 pounds of hamburger at a price of $1.49 per pound and 4.5 pounds of chicken at $1.19 per pound. Adam paid the clerk with a twenty-dollar bill.

13. Which arithmetic expression shows how to calculate Adam's change.

a) $20 − ($1.19 × 3.5) − ($1.49 × 4.5)
b) $20 − ($1.49 × 3.5) + ($1.19 × 4.5)
c) $20 − ($1.49 × 3.5) − ($1.19 × 4.5)

14. Use your calculator to find the value of the arithmetic expression you chose in problem #13.

Calculators with Algebra and Geometry

15. As shown below, Edna's back yard is in the shape of a rectangle. Use the Pythagorean Theorem to find the distance (d) between the corners marked A and B. Express your answer to the nearest foot.

Hint: $d = \sqrt{78^2 + 46^2}$

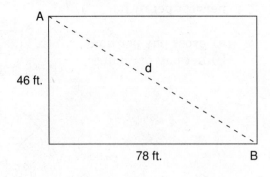

16. Fran works in a sheet metal shop that builds custom-made containers. She recently built the gasoline tank shown below.

a) Using the volume formula $V = lwh$, determine the container's volume to the nearest 10th cubic foot.

b) Knowing that 1 cubic foot holds about 7.5 gallons, how many gallons of gas can this tank hold?

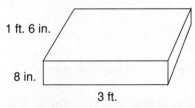

Hint: 6 in = .5 ft.
8 in. ≈ .67 ft.

ANSWER KEY

CALCULATOR BASICS

Page 4

Answers will vary. For calculators similar to the example on page 2, the answers are as follows:

1. Solar powered
2. The (ON/OFF) key
3. 0.
4. eight digits, 1 through 8
5. Press (C) once.
6. 99,999,999

Page 5

1. 2.57; 17.81; 20.56; 0.49; 0.08; 0.10
2. 4.19; 6.12
3. 0.27; 0.42
4. 0.04; 0.08
5. 1.06; 2.07

MORE ABOUT DISPLAYED NUMBERS

Page 7

A.
1. 2,450
2. 875 (no comma)
3. 4,056
4. 39,450
5. 1,832
6. 29,609

B.
1. $18.32 (no comma)
2. $2,471.60
3. $649.09 (no comma)
4. $5,038.18

C.
1. b) three hundred forty
2. c) nine hundred
3. c) three dollars and seven cents
4. a) twenty cents

D.
1. 95.
2. 243.
3. 3529.
4. 8406.
5. 15.82
6. 204.09

FUN WITH YOUR CALCULATOR MAKING THE DISPLAY SPEAK!

Page 8

1. O, I, Z, E, h, S, g, L, B
2. O, I, E
3. *hi, she, oil*
4. Some examples are *he, go, is,* and *hi.*
5. Some examples are *oil, she, his, bog,* and *log.*

ADDING TWO NUMBERS

Page 11

A.
1. (8)(+)(4)(=)
2. (3)(9)(+)(1)(7)(=)
3. (2)(0)(6)(3)(+)(9)(8)(9)(=)
4. (5)(·)(0)(9)(+)(4)(·)(2)(6)(=)
5. (1)(2)(8)(+)(8)(9)(=)
6. (7)(·)(9)(0)(+)(3)(·)(7)(8)(=)
7. (3)(5)(+)(1)(4)(=)
8. (1)(5)(7)(+)(6)(1)(=)
9. (5)(2)(0)(9)(+)(2)(4)(0)(0)(=)
10. (4)(·)(5)(0)(+)(6)(·)(1)(2)(=)

B.
1. 59; 657; 2,822
2. $1.65; $55.07; $415.74
3. 5,418 pounds

KEYING ERRORS

Page 12

A.
1. (2)(7)(+)(1)(8)(=)
2. (3)(9)(+)(2)(6)(=)
3. (1)(5)(3)(÷)(8)(9)(=)
4. (1)(6)(7)(+)(·)(4)(9)(=)
5. (8)(5)(+)(3)(2)(=)

B.

	Wrong Key	Double Keying	Transposed Digits
1.		✔	
2.			✔
3.	✔		
4.			✔
5.	✔		

DECIDING WHEN TO USE A CALCULATOR

Page 13

1. 6	3. 9	5. 7	7. 8
2. 13	4. 11	6. 13	8. 17
9. 50	11. 97	13. 99	15. 88
10. 91	12. 74	14. 106	16. 133
17. 469	19. 757	21. 879	23. $6.68
18. 1,127	20. 1,125	22. $1,413	24. $11.51

Answers will vary on categorizing answers. Many students, though, will choose to do the odd-numbered problems in their heads or with pencil and paper. These problems involve no carrying. Many students prefer to do carrying problems with a calculator, especially when more than single-digit problems are involved.

ADDING THREE OR MORE NUMBERS

Page 15

A.
1. (1)(2)(+)(9)(+)(8)(=)
2. (3)(5)(+)(2)(7)(+)(9)(=)
3. (1)(·)(5)(3)(+)(·)(9)(4)(+)(·)(5)(8)(=)

B.
1. 80; $6.71; 151
2. 110; $7.26; 336; $544; $283.24
3. $12.72

C. Problems 3, 4, 5, and 8 are incorrect.
3. $12.98
4. $635
5. 390
8. 8,001

SUBTRACTING TWO OR MORE NUMBERS

Page 17

A.
1. (5)(9)(−)(2)(8)(=)
2. (8)(6)(−)(4)(9)(=)
3. (5)(0)(8)(−)(2)(1)(7)(=)
4. (1)(0)(·)(0)(0)(−)(7)(·)(9)(2)(=)
5. (8)(·)(0)(0)(−)(3)(·)(1)(1)(=)

B. Incorrect problems are 1, 3, and 5.

C.
1. 2; 15; 16; $.60
2. 15; 34; 91
3. $2.92; $11.40
4. 1,269 pounds
5. $6.62

Page 18

A. 1. mental skills   4. calculator skills
2. mental skills   5. mental skills
3. mental skills

Page 19

B. 1. A   **C.** Answers will vary
2. larger numbers

THE IMPORTANCE OF ESTIMATING

Page 21

A. 1.

90	50	90
+ 70	+ 30	− 40
160	80	50

2.

500	900	$700
− 200	+ 100	− 300
300	1,000	$400

3.

5,000	8,000	12,000
+ 2,000	+ 5,000	− 8,000
7,000	13,000	4,000

B. 1. d) 90   3. a) 50   5. c) 700
2. e) 60   4. b) 100

ESTIMATION WITH CALCULATOR ADDITION AND SUBTRACTION

Pages 22–23

A. 1. b) $3.81   3. c) 48 inches
2. c) 8,019   4. a) $10.77

B. Estimates will vary. Example answers are given below.

1.

Exact	Estimate
397	400
207	200
+ 288	+ 300
892 calories	900 calories

2.

Exact	Estimate
407	400
+ 289	+ 300
696 miles	700 miles

3.

Exact	Estimate
407	400
− 289	− 300
118 miles	100 miles

4.

Exact	Estimate
$60.00	$60.00
− 3.89	− 4.00
$56.11	$56.00

5.

Exact	Estimate
91	90
− 49	− 50
42	40

6.

Exact	Estimate
$89.96	$90.00
38.75	40.00
+ 48.89	+ 50.00
$177.60	$180.00

SPOTLIGHT ON CONSUMERS ORDERING FROM A MENU

Page 24

1. No. The total cost of the meal is $7.52. He has only $7.00.
2. $11.93
3. $.62. Cost of meal = $3.43. If she spent a total of $4.05, she left $.62 in tax and tip. $4.05 − .62 = $3.43

SPOTLIGHT ON THE WORKPLACE KEEPING A MILEAGE RECORD

Page 25

1. **Daily Mileage**

Mon	382
Tue	407
Wed	354
Thu	430
Fri	288
Sat	376
Sun	529
TOTAL	2,766

2. WEEKLY TOTAL: 2,766 miles
3. a) Sat–Sun = 905 miles
   b) Mon–Fri = 1,861 miles

SPOTLIGHT ON CONSUMERS BALANCING A CHECKBOOK

Page 26

1 and 2 (See completed register below.)

RECORD ALL CHARGES OR CREDITS THAT AFFECT YOUR ACCOUNT

Number	Date	Description of Transaction	Payment/Debit (−)	✔ T	Fee (If Any) (−)	Deposit/Credit (+)	Balance $	
							568	43
202	6/1	North Street Apartments	$ 325 00	✓	$	$	243	43
203	6/4	Amy's Market	29 74				213	69
204	6/8	Import Auto Repair	109 66	✓			104	03
	6/15	Payroll Deposit				442 45	546	48
205	6/19	Value Pharmacy	13 29	✓			533	19
206	6/21	Gazette Times	8 75				524	44
207	6/23	Nelson's	39 83	✓			484	61
208	6/24	Hi-Ho Foods	63 79	✓			420	82
209		−VOID−						
210	6/25	Video Center	7 50	✓			413	32
	6/26	Check Reorder Charge	6 50				406	82
	6/30	Payroll Deposit				442 45	849	27
211	6/30	Washington Power	84 35	✓			764	92

REMEMBER TO RECORD AUTOMATIC PAYMENTS/DEPOSITS ON DATE AUTHORIZED

Page 27

Step 1. (See completed register above)
Step 2.

Check #203 $29.74
Check #206   + 8.75
              $38.49

Step 3. 06/30 Statement Balance $797.91
                                − 38.49
                              $759.42

Step 4. 06/30 Register Balance $764.92
Bank Service Charge   − 5.50
                                $759.42

Step 5. The amounts computed in Steps 3 and 4 are both equal to $759.42.

Page 29

A. 1. ⑦⑥⊗④⓪⊜

2. ①⓪⑥⊗⑧⑧⊜

3. ⑨·⓪④⊗⑦⊜

B. 1. a)

Exact	Estimate
48	50
× 32	× 30
1,536	1,500

b)

Exact	Estimate
67	70
× 59	× 60
3,953	4,200

c)

Exact	Estimate
88	90
× 19	× 20
1,672	1,800

2. a)

Exact	Estimate
192	200
× 57	× 60
10,944	12,000

b)

Exact	Estimate
289	300
× 32	× 30
9,248	9,000

c)

Exact	Estimate
206	200
× 74	× 70
15,244	14,000

C. 1. 280; 912; 1,955 3. $140.70; $254.80; $937.62

2. 6,216; 2,002; 98,298 4. $85.44

Page 31

A. 1. dividend = 152; divisor = 19

①⑤②÷①⑨⊜

2. dividend = $19.68; divisor = 8

①⑨·⑥⑧÷⑧⊜

B. 1. Exact: 143 ÷ 11 = 13; 153 ÷ 9 = 17; 187 ÷ 11 = 17
Estimate: 140 ÷ 10 = 14; 150 ÷ 10 = 15; 190 ÷ 10 = 19

2. Exact: 418 ÷ 19 = 22; 693 ÷ 21 = 33; 288 ÷ 18 = 16
Estimate: 400 ÷ 20 = 20; 700 ÷ 20 = 35; 300 ÷ 20 = 15

C. 1. 45; 26; $48; $61

2. 32 tables

3. $8.25

Pages 32–33

A. 1. b) division: 31 3. a) multiplication: $5.88

2. a) multiplication: 128 4. b) division: 32

B. Estimates may vary. Example estimates are given.

1. Estimate: $5.00 × 40 = $200.00
Exact: $4.89 × 39 = $190.71

2. Estimate: $2,000,000 ÷ 10 = $200,000
Exact: $1,972,800 ÷ 9 = $219,200

3. Estimate: 4,000 ÷ 20 = 200
Exact: 3,914 ÷ 19 = 206

4. Estimate: 7,000 × $5.00 = $35,000.00
Exact: 7,090 × $4.75 = $33,677.50

C. 1. $168 × 52 = $8,736 3. $274 ÷ 40 = $6.85

2. $274 × 52 = $14,248 4. $14,508 ÷ 52 = $279

Pages 34–35

1. cost of skirts = 3 × $14.89 = $44.67
change = $50.00 − $44.67 = $5.33

2. eggs in each case = 24 × 12 = 288
cases used = 1,728 ÷ 288 = 6

3. $7.59 ($5.75 + $.23 × 8)

4. $60.75 ($14.75 × 3 + $8.25 × 2)

5. 11 (subtract 119 from 405 and divide by 26)

6. $1,363.09 (subtract the Total, $13,920.19, from $15,283.28)

Page 36

1. 1. $149.40 5. $123.92

2. $199.95 6. $97.74

3. $62.55 7. $154.40

4. $150.96

2. TOTAL PURCHASE = $938.92

3. $876.37 ($938.92 − $62.55)

Page 37

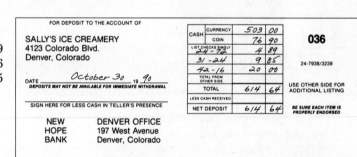

Page 38

1. a) $0.09 2. a) $0.24 3. (a) $0.07)
b) $0.08) b) $0.25 b) $0.08
c) $0.10 c) $0.23) c) $0.09

Page 39

1. Home Foods: $14.35 for 15 pounds

2. Henry's: $12.43 for 12 quarts

Page 41

1. R = D ÷ T = 182 ÷ 14 = 13 mph
2. D = RT = 49 × 7 = 343 miles
3. T = D ÷ R = 3,255 ÷ 620 = 5.25 hours
   or 5 hours 15 minutes
4. D = RT = 65 × 9 = 585 miles
5. Pam drove for 13 − 2 = 11 hours
   R = D ÷ T = 572 ÷ 11 = 52 mph
6. T = D ÷ R = 275 ÷ 55 = 5 hours
   8:00 A.M. + 5 hours = 1:00 P.M.
7. Erik wants to drive for 5 hours.
   R = D ÷ T = 265 ÷ 5 = 53 mph

CALCULATOR DIVISION WITH A REMAINDER

Page 43

A. Displayed Answer	Whole Number	Remainder
1. 15.75	15	.75
2. 42.75	42	.75
3. 41.6	41	.6
4. 36.625	36	.625
5. 118.66666	118	.66666

B. 1. 203 ÷ 12 = 16.916666
      Erwin will make 17 trips.
   2. $17.87 ÷ 3 = $5.9566666
      Sammy's share is $5.96.
   3. 23 ÷ 6 = 3.8333333
      Joe will need 4 display cases.

FINDING THE VALUE OF A REMAINDER

Page 45

A. Step 1. 598 ÷ 27 = 22.148148
   Step 2. 22 × 27 = 594
   Step 3. 598 − 594 = 4
   Whole number remainder = 4

B. 1. 15 r 3
   2. 9 r 17
   3. 18 r 11
   4. 39 r 5

C. 1. 114 ÷ 12 = 9.5
      The last load will contain 6 cubic yards.
   2. 3,185 ÷ 350 = 9.1
      She drove 35 miles on the final day.

Page 46

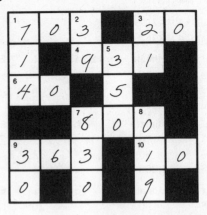

INTRODUCING DECIMALS

Page 49

A. 1. five hundredths
   2. five tenths
   3. five millionths
   4. five thousandths
   5. five hundred-thousandths
   6. five ten-thousandths

B. 1. c) 206 thousandths
   2. c) 47 thousandths
   3. a) 7 tenths
   4. a) 15 hundredths
   5. b) 9 thousandths
   6. b) 8 hundredths

C. 1. 1 ÷ 8 = 0.125
      b) 125 thousandths
   2. 9 ÷ 100 = 0.09
      b) 9 hundredths
   3. 30 ÷ 8 = 3.75
      b) 3 and 75 hundredths
   4. 5 ÷ 16 = 0.3125
      c) 3,125 ten-thousandths
   5. 20 ÷ 80 = 0.25
      c) 25 hundredths
   6. 245 ÷ 56 = 4.375
      a) 4 and 375 thousandths

ROUNDING DECIMAL FRACTIONS

Page 51

A. 1. $0.30
   2. $1.00
   3. $7.90
   4. $0.60
   5. $3.60
   6. $4.10

B. 1. 3.5; 3.46
   2. 14.4; 14.38
   3. 38.9; 38.95
   4. 40.1; 40.05
   5. 8.01; 8.007
   6. 24.00; 24.005
   7. 90.83; 90.831
   8. 72.38; 72.385

C. 1. 1.2307692 ≈ 1.2; 1.375 ≈ 1.4; 3.4285714 ≈ 3.4
   2. $1.9375 ≈ $1.94; 1.875 ≈ 1.88; $1.8888888 ≈ $1.89
   3. 1.4375 ≈ 1.438; 2.0454545 ≈ 2.045; 2.2857142 ≈ 2.286

D. 1. 33 ÷ 7 = 4.7142857 ≈ 4.71 inches
   2. 2.54 × 36 = 91.44 ≈ 91.4 centimeters

TERMINATING AND REPEATING DECIMALS

Page 53

A. 1. 1.25 terminating
   2. 0.333 . . . repeating
   3. 0.1515 . . . repeating
   4. 0.875 terminating

B. 1. 1.5454545
      repeating digits: .54 . . .
   2. 1.3333333
      repeating digits: .3 . . .
   3. 2.5555555
      repeating digits: .5 . . .
   4. 0.2424242
      repeating digits: .24 . . .

Pages 54–55

A. 1. ■ 2. ⬡ 3. ⊖ 4. ▢

B. 1. eight 2. go 3. smallest 4. mo

C. 1. 21 2. x 3. 13 4. U

D. 1. 46,046
       52,052
       28,028
      *34,034
      *16,016

   3. 222
       333
       444
      *555
      *777

   2. 1.1111111
       1.2222222
       1.3333333
      *1.4444444
      *1.6666666

   4. 0.3636363
       0.3939393
       0.4242424
      *0.4545454
      *0.5151515

E. 1. ÷ $510 ÷ 12 = $42.50
   2. + $48,795 + $17,980 = $66,775
   3. − 236 − 199 = 37 pounds
   4. × 22 × 16 = 352 miles
   5. ÷ 142 ÷ 5 = 28.4 pounds

Page 57

A. 1. 1.36; .99; 3.95
   2. .16; 2.5; 11.65

B. 1. a)
Exact	Estimate
8.3	8
+ 5.6	+ 6
13.9	14

b)
Exact	Estimate
9.7	10
+ 6.5	+ 7
16.2	17

c)
Exact	Estimate
6.3	6
+ 7.1	+ 7
13.4	13

2. a)
Exact	Estimate
25.8	30
+ 13.6	+ 10
39.4	40

b)
Exact	Estimate
75.60	80
+ 24.83	+ 20
100.43	100

c)
Exact	Estimate
27.85	30
+ 12.4	+ 10
40.25	40

3. a)
Exact	Estimate
328.65	300
211.06	200
+ 123	+ 100
662.71	600

b)
Exact	Estimate
547.69	500
243.63	200
+ 181.8	+ 200
973.12	900

c)
Exact	Estimate
900	900
375.8	400
+ 245.18	+ 200
1,520.98	1,500

Page 57 (continued)

C. 1. 37; 95; $204
   2. 387; 318; $58

D. 3.74 inches

Page 59

A. 1. .81
   2. .11
   3. .035

B. 1. 0.23; 0.175; 0.019
   2. 0.044; 0.01; 0.026

C. 1. 0.153
   2. $4.65
   3. $0.70
   4. 5.4°F

Pages 60–61

A. 1. b) 4.83 (3 + 2 = 5)
   2. a) 1.41 (6 − 5 = 1)
   3. c) $21.90 ($60 − $40 = $20)

B. Estimates may vary.

   1. Estimate: 14 − 12 = 2 seconds
      Exact: 14.26 − 11.89 = 2.37 seconds
   2. Estimate: 30 − 28 = 2 miles per gallon
      Exact: 30.2 − 27.8 = 2.4 miles per gallon
   3. Estimate: $12.00 + $2.00 = $14.00
      Exact: $11.88 + $2.29 = $14.17
   4. Estimate: 4 − 3 = 1 mile
      Exact: 4.18 − 3.29 = .89 mile
   5. Estimate: 21 − 19 = 2 gallons
      Exact: 20.7 − 18.9 = 1.8 gallons
   6. Estimate: .9 − .6 = .3 inch
      Exact: .9375 − .625 = .3125 inch

Page 63

A. 46.8; 7.71; 5.628; 72.05; .7688

B. 1. a)
Exact	Estimate
6.8	7
× 4.2	× 4
28.56	28

b)
Exact	Estimate
8.12	8
× .94	× 1
7.6328	8

c)
Exact	Estimate
4.03	4
× 2.1	× 2
8.463	8

2. a)
Exact	Estimate
10.3	10
× 5.9	× 6
60.77	60

b)
Exact	Estimate
12.9	13
× 1.09	× 1
14.061	13

c)
Exact	Estimate
15.4	15
× 2.19	× 2
33.726	30

C. 1. 144; 454.2
   2. 345; 554.4
   3. $111.32; $283.89
   4. $20.32

Page 65

A. 1. dividend (6.54) divisor 3.1
   2. dividend (8) divisor 2.7

B. 1. b) 8 (48 ÷ 6 = 8)   3. b) 10 (100 ÷ 10 = 10)
   2. a) 8 (32 ÷ 4 = 8)   4. c) 7 (56 ÷ 8 = 7)

C. 1. 44.8; 24.3; 50.4; 9.5
   2. 33.91; $3.09; $23.81; 2.41
   3. $3.68

ESTIMATING WITH CALCULATOR MULTIPLICATION AND DIVISION

Pages 66–67

A. Example estimates are given in parentheses.

   1. c) between $6 and $8 ($63 ÷ 9 = $7)
   2. b) between 250 and 350 (30 × 10 = 300)
   3. b) between $48 and $52 ($7 × 7 = $49)
   4. c) between 26 and 32 (3 × 10 = 30)
   5. a) between $3 and $4 ($15 ÷ 5 = $3)

B. 1. Estimate: $1.20 ÷ 3 = $.40
     Exact: $1.19 ÷ 2.9 = $.41 (to nearest cent)
   2. Estimate: 60 ÷ 20 = 3 pounds
     Exact: 59.8 ÷ 22 = 2.7 pounds (to nearest tenth
       pound)
   3. Estimate: 1 × 8 = 8 inches
     Exact: .9375 × 8 = 7.5 inches
   4. Estimate: 50 × 8 = 400 pounds
     Exact: 48 × 8.3 = 398.4 pounds

C. 1. $5.44 × 40 = $217.60
   2. $5.44 × 1.5 = $8.16
   3. $217.60 + (5 × $8.16) = $258.40
   4. $245.50 ÷ 40 = $6.14 (to nearest cent)

SPOTLIGHT ON CONSUMERS FINDING AN AVERAGE

Page 68

1. $115.25
2. 175
3. $14.37 (to nearest cent)

SPOTLIGHT ON THE WORKPLACE INTERPRETING A PAYCHECK STUB

Page 69

A. 1. a) subtract $539.57 from $684.80
     b) add $79.24, $14.27, and $51.72
   2. $8,217.60
   3. $79.24

B. 1. $145.23 ($684.80 − $539.57)
   2. 12 pay periods ($8,217.60 ÷ $684.80)
   3. a) $8.72 (to nearest cent; $684.80 ÷ 78.5)
     b) $6.87 (to nearest cent; $539.57 ÷ 78.5)
   4. $1,344.72 ($51.72 × 26)

SPOTLIGHT ON CONSUMERS COMPARING COSTS OF CHILDCARE

Page 70

	At Super Kids	At Huggy Bear
1.	$260.95	$302
2.	$485.90	$534
3.	$746.85	$836

4. Super Kids would be $89.15 less for three months.

SPOTLIGHT ON THE WORKPLACE COMPARING ANNUAL CAR COSTS

Page 71

	Chevrolet	Ford
1.	$372.76	$410.32
2.	$2,539.07	$2,657.25
3.	706	857
4.	$826.02	$1,002.69
5.	$59.85	$59.85
6.	$885.87	$1,062.54
7.	$3,424.94	$3,719.79

REVIEWING COMMON FRACTIONS

Page 73

A. 1. 0.76; $\frac{5}{8}$; 0.4; 0.865   2. $\frac{2}{3}$; $\frac{9}{17}$; $\frac{2}{3}$; $\frac{8}{10}$

B. 1. $\frac{3}{8}$ of a dollar
   2. Bit #3: $\frac{13}{64}$ inch
   3. No

CALCULATIONS WITH FRACTIONS

Page 75

1. c) $8\frac{5}{24}$ 3. a) $6\frac{2}{35}$ 5. $.75 per pound
2. b) $14\frac{2}{3}$ 4. b) $2\frac{4}{15}$

FUN WITH YOUR CALCULATOR TIC-TAC-TOE

Page 76

Letters indicate which problem has an answer that matches the answer appearing within each square.

h	n	k
l	b	c
j	f	p

OVERVIEW OF PERCENT

Page 79

1. b) percent, division
2. a) part, multiplication
3. c) whole, division

*Page 81

1. 18, 84, $2.04, 66
2. 368, $41.40, 274, $1.42
3. $.02, .595, $1.65, 2.108
4. 45, $174, 135, $112
5. $36.54 (②④③·⑥⓪×①⑤%)
6. $11.50 (④⑥⓪×②·⑤%)
7. $20.93 (⑤⑨⑧×③·⑤%)

*Page 83

1. 20%
2. 80%
3. 38%
4. 40%
5. 60%
6. 32%
7. 50%
8. 51.7%
9. 25%; 60%; 45%; 70%; 40%
10. 37.5%; 31.3%; 33.3%; 9.4%; 66.7%
11. 14% (④②÷③⓪⓪%)
12. 40% (②÷⑤%)

*Page 85

1. 268
2. 1,000
3. $28
4. 150
5. 250
6. $2,000
7. $40
8. $2,500
9. 20 pounds (⑥÷③⓪%)
10. $660 (⑨·⑨⓪÷①·⑤%)
11. $18 (①②·⑥⓪÷⑦⓪%)

*Page 87

1. 99¢ per pound (⑨⓪+①⓪%)
2. 60,264 (④⑧⑥⓪⓪+②④%)
3. $12,290.28 (①③④③②−⑧·⑤%)
4. $129.22 (①⑧④·⑥⓪−③⓪%)
5. $28.29 (②④·⑥⓪+①⑤%)
6. $72.80 (⑤⑥+③⓪%)
7. $112.35 (①④⑨·⑧⓪−②⑤%)
8. $12.74 (①④·①⑥−①⓪%)

*Pages 88–89

A. 1. **b)** exactly 42 (100% means all.)
   2. **a)** less than 100% (18 is a part of 24.)
   3. **c)** more than $860 (Shelley is getting a raise.)
   4. **a)** less than 100% (14 is a part of 34.)

B. 1. whole; $320 (④⑧÷①⑤%)
   2. part; 15,570 (③④⑥⓪⓪×④⑤%)
   3. percent decrease; 60 (⑦⑤−②⓪%)
   4. percent; 37% (④②⑥÷①①⑤④%)
   5. percent decrease; $67.20 (⑧④−②⓪%)
   6. whole; $36.00 (②⑧·⑧⓪÷⑧⓪%)
   7. percent; 10% (①·②⑤÷①②·⑤⓪%)
      since $12.50 − $11.25 = $1.25
   8. percent; 13% (②⓪÷①⑤⓪%)
      since 150 − 130 = 20
   9. percent decrease; 144 pounds (①⑤⓪−④%)

Page 90

Name	M	T	W	T	F	S	S	① Total Hours	② Regular Hours	③ Overtime Hours
Allen	8.0	8.0	9.0	9.5	7.5	3.0		45	40	5
Cook	8.0	9.5	6.5	9.0	8.5	2.5	2.5	46.5	40	6.5
Dart	7.5	9.0	5.5	7.5	6.5			36	36	0
Franks		8.5	7.5	8.5	9.0	8.5	3.5	45.5	40	5.5
Norris	9.0	8.5	8.0	5.5	7.5	8.5		47	40	7

*Page 91

Name	① Regular Hours	② Regular Pay Rate	③ Total Regular Pay	④ Overtime Hours	⑤ Overtime Pay Rate	⑥ Total Overtime Pay	⑦ Total Pay	⑧ Total % Withholding	⑨ Net Pay
Allen	40	$5.32	$212.80	5	$7.98	$39.90	$252.70	14%	$217.32
Cook	40	$5.32	$212.80	6.5	$7.98	$51.87	$264.67	14%	$227.62
Dart	36	$6.28	$226.08	0	$9.42	0	$226.08	16%	$189.91
Franks	40	$6.48	$259.20	5.5	$9.72	$53.46	$312.66	16%	$262.63
Norris	40	$7.94	$317.60	7	$11.91	$83.37	$400.97	18%	$328.80

Total Regular Hours For All Workers **196**
(ADD COLUMN 1)
Total Overtime Hours For All Workers **24**
(ADD COLUMN 4)
Total Regular Pay For All Workers **$1,228.48**
(ADD COLUMN 3)

Total Net Pay For All Workers **$1,226.28**
(ADD COLUMN 9)
Total Overtime Pay For All Workers **$228.60**
(ADD COLUMN 6)

* On some calculators, you may need to press (=) after (%) to complete the calculation.

Page 93

A. 1. .417 year
   2. 3.083 years
   3. 4.583 years

B. 1. $450 (I = $2,500 × 6% × 3)
   2. $540 (I = $1,500 × 18% × 2)
   3. $88.59 (I = $750 × 5.25% × 2.25)
   4. $427.12 (Interest = $375 × 5.75% × 2.417)
      (Total = $375.00 + $52.12)
   5. $767.81 (Interest = $650 × 14.5% × 1.25)
      (Total = $650 + $117.81)

SPOTLIGHT ON CONSUMERS
PERCENT AND A FAMILY BUDGET

Page 95

1. The percents are as follows:
   Housing 32%
   Other 5%
   Clothing 4%
   Transportation 16%
   Food 29%
   Savings 3%
   Medical Care 11%

2. $2,339.84
3. 47%
4. 23%
5. 5%
6. $183
7. $359.40
8. $562.50

FUN WITH YOUR CALCULATOR
BRAIN TEASERS

Page 96

A. 1. d   **3.** c   **5.** b
   2. a   **4.** e

B. 1. 100   **4.** 100   **7.** 200
   2. 50   **5.** 200   **8.** 150
   3. 5   **6.** 20   **9.** 15

BECOMING FAMILIAR WITH YOUR
CALCULATOR'S MEMORY

Page 99

1. e   **3.** a   **5.** c
2. d   **4.** b

UNDERSTANDING ARITHMETIC
EXPRESSIONS

Page 101

   1. Add 26 and 14; then subtract 9.
   2. Multiply 13 × 4; then subtract 18.
   3. Divide 64 by 8; then add 11.
   4. Multiply 9 × 8; then add 21.
   5. Divide 56 by 7; then subtract this quotient from 60.
   6. Add the product of 7 × 6 to the product of 8 × 3.
   7. Subtract the product of 7 × 6 from the product of 9 × 8.
   8. Add 7 and 6; then multiply the sum by 9.
   9. Subtract 10 from 12; then multiply the difference by 8.
   10. Subtract 12 from 30; then divide the difference by 6.

GAINING CONFIDENCE WITH ARITHMETIC
EXPRESSIONS

Pages 104–105

A. 1. 25 (2 8 − 1 7 + 1 4 =)
   2. $17.73 (1 2 . 4 3 + 9 . 3 6 − 4 . 0 6 =)
   3. 181 (3 9 6 − 2 0 9 − 4 3 + 3 7 =)
   4. 184 (2 0 7 + 1 1 1 − 7 3 − 6 1 =)
   5. $8.25 (1 3 . 4 6 − 2 . 0 9 − 3 . 1 2 =)
   6. $1.12 (4 . 2 5 − 2 . 1 9 − 1 . 1 8 + . 2 4 =)

B. 1. 600 (4 3 + 7 × 1 2 =)
   2. 7 (5 6 − 2 8 ÷ 4 =)
   3. $20.61 (4 . 5 6 + 2 . 3 1 × 3 =)
   4. 6 (4 5 + 2 8 − 1 9 ÷ 9 =)
   5. 392 (6 3 − 3 5 × 1 4 =)
   6. 80 (2 9 − 1 3 × 5 =)
   7. $4.55 (6 . 2 5 + 2 . 8 5 ÷ 2 =)
   8. 114 (1 1 2 + 1 0 9 + 1 2 1 ÷ 3 =)

*C. 1. 210 (1 5 6 M+ 1 8 × 3 M+ MR)
   2. 17 (9 M+ 1 0 4 ÷ 1 3 M+ MR)
   3. 31.3 (1 8 . 7 M+ 4 . 2 × 3 M+ MR)
   4. 67 (7 . 2 × 6 M+ 3 . 4 × 7 M+ MR)
   5. 138 (8 4 × 3 M+ 5 7 × 2 M− MR)
   6. 25 (3 7 M+ 3 × 4 M− MR)
   7. 6 (1 5 M+ 1 5 3 ÷ 1 7 M− MR)
   8. 12 (2 7 . 6 M+ 7 . 8 × 2 M− MR)
   9. $29.51 (3 . 7 9 × 4 M+ 2 . 8 7 × 5 M+ MR)
   10. $5.38 (5 0 M+ 1 3 . 4 9 × 2 M− 5 . 8 8 × 3 M− MR)

*D. 1. $6.88 (7 . 5 6 + 2 . 8 9 − 3 . 5 7 =)
   2. $9.35 (8 . 2 9 − 6 . 4 2 × 5 =)
   3. $17.83 (2 . 4 9 × 3 M+ 5 . 1 8 × 2 M+ MR)
   4. $5.12 (1 0 − 2 . 9 9 − 1 . 8 9 =)
   5. 1,122 (1 4 3 + 2 3 1 × 3 =)
   6. 65.1 (5 . 7 + 3 . 6 × 7 =)
   7. $5.07 (2 7 . 4 6 − 1 7 . 3 2 ÷ 2 =)

* On some calculators, you may have to press (=) before you press (M+) or (M−).

D. 8. $14.44 ((1)(4)(·)(6)(8)(+)(1)(6)(·)(2)(0)
(+)(1)(2)(·)(4)(4)(÷)(3)(=))

  9. $11.60 ((5)(·)(8)(9)(−)(2)(·)(9)(9)(×)(4)(=))

  10. $19.03 ((2)(5)(M+)(5)(·)(2)(5)(×)(3)
(M−)(4)(·)(8)(9)(×)(2)(M+)(MR))

CALCULATOR POWER IN MULTISTEP WORD PROBLEMS

Page 107

A. 1. **b)** $25.00 − $14.79 − $4.99 = $5.22
  2. **c)** ($3.95 + $1.99 + $1.99) ÷ 3 = $2.64
  3. **c)** $152.90 − $41.49 + $85.00 = $196.41
  4. **b)** ($334.80 − $50.00) ÷ 8 = $35.60
  5. **a)** (9 + 8) × 11.5 = 195.5
  6. **b)** (3 × 5) + (2 × 3) = 21

Page 108

B. 1. $84.29 − $18.75 + $125.94 = $191.48
  2. $241.85 + $51.38 − $53.00 = $240.23
  3. (1.9 + 1.9) × 5 = 19 miles
  4. 20 − (4.3 × 4) = 2.8 pounds
  5. ($329.99 − $44.99) ÷ 3 = $95.00
  6. ($1.75 × 6.4) − ($1.08 × 4.5) = $6.34
  7. (182 + 175 + 193) ÷ 3 = 183

SPECIAL MULTISTEP PROBLEM: FINDING PERCENT INCREASE OR DECREASE

***Page 109**

A. 1. 12.5% ((6)(·)(3)(0)(−)(5)(·)(6)(0)
(÷)(5)(·)(6)(0)(%))

  2. 29% ((6)(2)(8)(0)(0)(−)(4)(8)(6)(0)(0)
(÷)(4)(8)(6)(0)(0)(%))

  3. 25% ((1)(·)(5)(−)(1)(·)(2)(÷)(1)(·)(2)(%))

B. 1. 27% ((3)(8)(·)(5)(0)(−)(2)(7)(·)(9)(5)
(÷)(3)(8)(·)(5)(0)(%))

  2. 15% ((7)(2)(6)(0)(0)(−)(6)(1)(7)(1)(0)
(÷)(7)(2)(6)(0)(0)(%))

  3. 40% ((1)(·)(2)(5)(−)(·)(7)(5)(÷)(1)(·)(2)(5)
(%))

TOPIC 1: POWERS

Page 113

1. 16; 0.16; 16.81; 64; 144
2. 125; 1,296; 8; 512; 6,561
3. 11.56; 2,015.1121; 84.64; 314.432; 2,687.3856
4. 4,096; 97.336; 2,401; 27; 133.6336

TOPIC 2: SQUARE ROOTS

Page 114

A. 1. $8 = \sqrt{64}$
  2. $13 = \sqrt{169}$
  3. $2.4 = \sqrt{5.76}$

B. 1. 15; 20; 30; 3.16; 4.47
  2. 4.8; 6.48; 3.95; .86; .3

Page 115

1. 145; 66.49; 95;
2. 5; 13.6; 91.65
3. 22.02; 7.91; 41.71

TOPIC 3: RIGHT TRIANGLES AND THE PYTHAGOREAN THEOREM

Page 117

A. Step 1. (5)(×)(5)(M+)   Step 3. (MR)
  Step 2. (8)(×)(8)(M+)   Step 4. (√)

B. 1. 12.2 feet ((7)(×)(7)(M+)(1)(0)(×)(1)(0)(M+)(MR)
(√))

  2. 13.9 feet ((5)(×)(5)(M+)(1)(3)(×)(1)(3)(M+)(MR)
(√))

  3. 44 yards ((3)(4)(×)(3)(4)(M+)(2)(8)(×)(2)(8)
(M+)(MR)(√))

  4. 7.5 miles ((6)(·)(5)(×)(6)(·)(5)(M+)(3)(·)(8)
(×)(3)(·)(8)(M+)(MR)(√))

TOPIC 4: WORKING WITH MEASUREMENT FORMULAS

Page 118

1. $P = 4s$; $P = 16.75$ inches
2. $P = 2(l + w)$; $P = 23.8$ miles
3. $C = 2\pi r$; $C = 31.4$ feet

Page 119

1. $A = lw$; $A = 8.7$ square feet
2. $A = b \times h \div 2$; $A = 13.5$ square yards
3. $A = \pi r^2$; $A = 75.4$ square inches

Page 120

1. $V = lwh$; $V = 31.5$ cubic inches
2. $V = s^3$; $V = 103.82$ cubic yards
3. $V = \pi r^2 h$; $V = 21.23$ cubic yards

CALCULATOR POWER IN MEASUREMENT WORD PROBLEMS

Page 121

1. Formula: $P = 2(l + w)$: Answer: 18.8 feet
2. Formula: $C = 2\pi r$; Answer: 88 feet
3. Formula: $A = \pi r^2$; Answer: 615 square feet
4. Formula: $A = \frac{1}{2} bh$; Answer: 6 square feet
5. Formula: $A = lw$; Answer: 3,358 square yards
6. Formula: $V = lwh$; Answer: 15 cubic feet
7. Formula: $V = \pi r^2 h$; Answer: 12,717 cubic feet

---

* On some calculators, you may need to press (=) to complete the calculation.

Page 123

1. $4,775.44   **Press Keys**

Ⓞ ⓪ ⑥ ÷ ③ + ① = × = = × ④ ⑤ ⓪ ⓪ =

2. $3,368.87   **Press Keys**

Ⓞ ① ④ ÷ ② + ① = × = = × ② ⑦ ⑤ ⓪ =

3. $8,843.18   **Press Keys**

Ⓞ ① ⑥ ÷ ② + ① = × = = =

× ⑥ ⑤ ⓪ ⓪ =

CALCULATOR SKILLS CHECKUP

Pages 124–126

1.

RECORD ALL CHARGES OR CREDITS THAT AFFECT YOUR ACCOUNT

Number	Date	Description of Transaction	Payment/Debit (−)	✓ T	Fee (If Any) (−)	Deposit/Credit (+)	Balance	
			$		$	$	641	90
309	7/6	Hillcrest Apartments	275 00				366	90
310	7/7	Value Food Store	19 85				347	05
311	7/10	Northern Power Co.	107 33				239	72
312		— VOID —						
313	7/14	Hair Palace	12 00				227	72
	7/16	Deposit Paycheck				342 61	570	33
314	7/18	2D Variety Store	27 93				542	40

REMEMBER TO RECORD AUTOMATIC PAYMENTS/DEPOSITS ON DATE AUTHORIZED

2.

WHOLESALE BATHROOM SUPPLIES

	Item #	Description	Quantity	Cost/Per	Total Amount
1.	A 241	Bath mat	14	18.45	$258.30
2.	B 647	Bath towel	29	10.98	$318.42
3.	D 832	Wall mirror	7	73.49	$514.43
4.	F 301	Shower Curtain	16	19.99	$319.84
5.	P 970	Window Curtain	8	48.75	$390.00
				Total Purchase	$1,800.99

3. Donnie's at $19.14
4. a) 22 trips; **b)** 192 bricks
5. $177
6. $4.98
7. $113.64
8. $1,624.48
9. a) $7.21; **b)** $5.79
10. 26%
11. $3,171
12. $618.70
13. c) $20 − ($1.49 × 3.5) − ($1.19 × 4.5)
14. $9.43
15. 91 ft.
16. a) 3.0 cubic ft.
     b) 22.5 gallons